NLP
BUSINESS
SUCCESS

ANDREW BRADBURY

KOGAN PAGE
BETTER MANAGEMENT SKILLS

YOURS TO HAVE AND TO HOLD
BUT NOT TO COPY

First published in 1997
Reprinted 1997, 1998

Kogan Page Limited
120 Pentonville Road
London N1 9JN

British Library Cataloguing in Publication Data
A CIP record for this book is available from the British Library.

ISBN 0 7494 2151 7

Typeset by BookEns Ltd., Royston, Herts.
Printed in England by Clays Ltd, St Ives plc

Contents

1. Introducing NLP   5
2. Points of View   12
3. Cultures, Values and Beliefs   16
4. Know What You Want to Get What You Want   20
5. Building Relationships   28
6. Talking Body Language   33
7. Follow the Leader   37
8. Give the Dog a New Name   39
9. When You Put It Like That ...   42
10. Clear Thinking or Gut Feeling?   48
11. Making Information Make Sense   50
12. Avoiding Resistance   55
13. Self-Management   57
14. Using Preferred Thinking Styles   61
15. Presentations   69
16. Discipline   71
17. Appraisals   76
18. Motivation   79
19. Negotiations   86
20. Sales   91
21. Meetings   96
22. Honesty   99

Basic NLP Terms Used in this Book   103
Select Bibliography   109
Further Reading from Kogan Page   110

CHAPTER 1
Introducing NLP

Winning ways

NLP — Neuro-Linguistic Programming — is one of the most powerful tools ever made available to the business community. The term 'neuro-linguistic' was coined by Alfred Korzybski (founder of the General Semantics movement) several decades ago, but NLP—developed by Bandler, Grinder *et al* – has gone far beyond Korzybski's original ideas to become what is probably the most comprehensive synthesis of modern psychological knowledge around today.

The name Neuro-Linguistic Programming breaks down into three parts:

- *Neuro* —   which covers what goes on in the brain and in the nervous system.
- *Linguistic* —   referring to the way that we use words, and how this affects our perceptions of, and relationship with, the external world.
- *Programming* —   an interactive process which allows us to make very precise choices about the way we think, speak and feel.

It could be said that standard management theory tends to be a bit like the scientist who discovered that bees 'cannot' fly (their wings are too small, their bodies are an aerodynamic nightmare, and so on). Likewise, there are plenty of ideas about what is wrong with management, but not many on 'how' to change things for the better.

NLP, on the other hand, is like the experienced bee-keeper who ignores the scientific view and goes on helping his bees to be as productive as possible.

In other words, NLP deals with things the way they *are* rather than getting bogged down in what *ought to be*. It offers an in-depth understanding of what really happens when we communicate, and the means to use that knowledge so as to maximise the effectiveness of any interpersonal transaction, be it sales, negotiation, a presentation, an appraisal or whatever.

People like people who are like themselves.

WIIFM – What's in it for me?

Any business person who has a grasp of the basic NLP concepts and techniques, and who learns how to utilise this information effectively, can expect to enjoy a significant improvement in all aspects of their business *and* social activities.

In practical terms, NLP shows you how to become more successful in business by:

- Setting effective goals, leading to more focused activity.
- Building good quality relationships with colleagues and business associates, replacing conflict with co-operation.
- Developing greater flexibility in the way that you respond to your environment, leading to more appropriate responses to the ever-changing demands of your business.
- Managing your mental activities, leading to greater self-control and more effective self-management.

One of the most basic concepts in NLP is: 'What one person can learn to do, anyone else can learn to do.' From its earliest days, NLP has been based on a process of 'modelling' successful people (as judged by their peers) in all walks of life.

Having modelled a person's behaviour, it is then possible to compare it with that of their less successful colleagues in order to spot the 'differences that make the difference'.

These variations are often very subtle, but once they have been identified, they can be adopted by other people who wish to enhance their own performance.

To put it quite simply, the basic NLP concept is: find out what works, then do it. This means that the techniques described in NLP are all based on what some people are already doing. You may already be using some of these skills without even recognising them for what they are. It is this lack of awareness that locks us into the predicament where what leads to success in one situation can lead to failure in another.

> We already have all the resources we need to deal with almost any situation in which we may find ourselves.

Influencing with integrity

Because they are rooted in proven success, these ideas and techniques are extremely powerful, and it may seem that there is a very real chance that they can be misused.

Quite right.

Just as you can use a hammer to build a beautiful boat, or hit your thumb, or bash somebody's head in, these techniques can be used for good or ill. But as Genie Laborde points out in her book *Influencing with Integrity*, there are clear penalties involved in using NLP in a manipulative manner:

- Resentment;
- Recrimination;
- Remorse;
- Revenge.

The reader is respectfully urged to heed this warning.

Using this book

The purpose of this book is to provide a *practical* guide to using NLP to achieve business excellence. As far as the layout is concerned, rather than repeat the same piece of information several times over, the basic details of the various NLP techniques and ideas are set out in Chapters 2–13. Chapters 14–21 discuss how NLP can be applied in various business situations. These chapters frequently refer back to the appropriate sections in Chapters 2–13. For example, wherever the subject of 'congruence' is referred to in Chapters 14–21 (in the chapter on Negotiations, for instance) the reader is simply referred back to the chapter on congruence in Chapters 2–13.

Chapters 2–13 each end with one or more *checkpoint actions* which will help you to build on the points covered in that chapter. This approach allows the information to be presented in a succinct manner that underlines in a practical way the highly integrated nature of NLP theory and practice.

Developing NLP skills

As you read through this book you will discover that it is very easy to pick up the basic ideas in NLP. Becoming proficient in the use of NLP techniques takes just a little longer. This process can be modelled as four levels of competence:

1. You don't know what you don't know.
2. You are very aware of what you don't know.
3. You are very aware of what you do know.
4. You can use your knowledge without thinking about it.

Let me illustrate the four levels by introducing you to an important NLP skill known as 'sensory acuity':

Level 1
Many readers may respond to that last sentence by asking what is meant by the term 'sensory acuity'. In other words, on this particular topic they are at Level 1, 'unconscious incompetence'.

In a business context, being able to recognise when you are at Level 1 on a given subject, and acting accordingly, are valuable skills in their own right.

Level 2

I now explain that the mind and the body are both parts of a single system. I go on to say that sensory acuity is the process of observing another person's physiological responses — changes in skin colour and in muscular tension and relaxation, etc — and that this gives you some insight into that person's mental activity. You might then think of someone blushing because they are embarrassed or clenching their jaw muscles because they are angry. You have begun to understand what sensory acuity is about, although you are still only aware of the most obvious examples of the body–mind link.

You have moved into Level 2: 'conscious incompetence'.

At this level NLP may *appear* to be no more than a set of tricks and techniques.

Level 3

After a time, while you still need to practise your skills, you will be able to spot the more subtle physical signals, although the process of observing and interpretation is still something you need to think about.

This is Level 3: 'conscious competence'.

At this level of expertise you will have begun to understand that there is far more to NLP than meets the eye.

Level 4

Finally, with practice, experience, and preferably with some professional tutoring, you will be able to respond to other people's behaviour in a highly effective, yet effortless manner.

You have reached Level 4: 'unconscious competence', where you are able to use your NLP skills to full effect as a natural and instinctive reaction to whatever situation you are in.

The choice is yours

In place of a checkpoint action for this chapter, I want to demonstrate the point I made earlier: everyone has the resources they need to cope with any situation.

How often have you heard someone say something like: 'He makes me so angry'? Probably too often to keep count, yet this is actually a completely false assessment of how other people's behaviour can affect us. After all, if it were really possible for another person to *make* me angry, that person, by definition, must have greater control over my emotions than me.

Our emotional reactions to the events around us are actually based on our *perceptions* of those events, and our perceptions, as we will see in a moment, are entirely under our own control.

As a very simple example of selective perception, the verb 'To speak one's mind' might be conjugated thus:

> I believe in being frank
> You are outspoken
> He is downright rude.

On a more serious level, if I am in control of my emotions, even under the most trying conditions, I am free to decide whether I will control the situation, or simply react. In order to make a choice, I must *know* what resources I have available to me, which is what this demonstration is about.

In order to do this exercise, you should read each step — *and carry out the required action* — before moving on to the next step.

Step 1
Think of a situation at work which, while not too serious, has caused you a certain degree of annoyance or irritation.

Recall the event as though you were watching a film (close your eyes if it helps). Watch the film, listen to the soundtrack — people talking and so on — and recall any feelings, both physical and emotional, which are part of the event. Watch the whole film before going on to Step 2.

Step 2
Next, think of a piece of music which you like and which is the complete opposite in mood to the event you recalled in Step 1. If several different pieces of music suggest themselves, select one piece in particular before moving to Step 3.

Step 3
Now run that film again, but this time include, as part of the soundtrack, the piece of music you selected in Step 2.
    Run the whole film before reading Step 4.

Step 4
Finally, run the film through one more time, *without* the music. Notice how your emotional feelings have changed − how the negative sensations have lessened, or even disappeared.

What you have just experienced is first-hand evidence of how your perceptions shape your feelings, and how you can control or, in NLP terms, *program* your perceptions, and thus your feelings, to produce a positive and beneficial state of mind.
    You have always had this resource, and may have used it many times (playing a favourite record to remind you of a special occasion, for example), without being conscious of it. Now you both have the resource *and* know how to use it.
    The rest of this book will show how various NLP techniques can be used to make you more positive and effective in every area of your business activities.

CHAPTER 2
Points of View

The map is not the territory

Our ability to interact with the external world is greatly influenced by our very restricted *conscious* abilities. For example, while we receive an estimated 2.4 million bits of information every minute (through our various senses) we can consciously handle only about 300–500 bits of information per minute. The remaining 2.35 million bits of information are filtered and dealt with at the *un*conscious level.

This process of abstracting a limited picture of the total reality in which we live is referred to in NLP as mapping or mapmaking. Not surprisingly, given such a mass of information, no two people ever have *exactly* the same map of any part of the external world. On the contrary, a single word can be the basis for two quite separate maps:

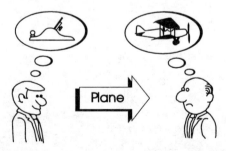

(Please note that the terms 'maps' and 'map making' are used throughout this chapter to refer to *mental* maps and the way we verbally describe them.)

Everyone has their own personal views of the world, their own 'maps of reality'. Even in this book there are certain things that will not tally with the experiences of every single reader.

Having said that, none of us can take the final step to maturity until we recognise the crucial difference between 'this is true/not true' and 'this is true/not true *for me*'.

At the end of Jane's presentation Bob criticised the way that she had used bullet points on some of her slides and numbering in the handout. 'If you use numbers in the notes then you *must* use numbers on your slides', he insisted, 'that's the proper way of conducting a lecture.'

Bob had clearly understood the relationship between the numbered notes and the bulleted slides, so it wasn't the numbering and bullets points *as such* that had caused the upset. The 'real problem' was that Jane's style was at odds with Bob's internal map of how a 'lecture' should be presented. Bob overlooked the fact that there were nearly 30 people at the presentation, each of whom had their own view of what constituted a 'good presentation'. Most of those people chose to put their personal views (if any) to one side in order to get the most out of the presentation.

By insisting that his map alone was valid Bob created an element of conflict, and reduced his ability to find the presentation useful, enjoyable or informative.

We need maps to guide us through unknown territory, but we must also be aware that even the best map is only a very rough guide to the landscape it represents:

A Word	**IS NOT**	**The THING it describes**
A Map		**The PLACE it depicts**
A Symbol		**The THING it represents**

The truth is that our knowledge, on any subject you care to name, will *always* be incomplete. Likewise, no matter how much care and thought we give it, we can never be totally accurate in our description of any person, thing, event or whatever. As one writer put it:

- Whatever we do or say, it is certain that we will be misunderstood – to some degree.
- Whatever we see or hear, it is certain we will misunderstand it – to some degree.
- We can never eliminate misunderstandings – but this should not deter us from striving to *minimise* them.

One very important way of making our communications more effective (and our relationships more harmonious) is by being constantly aware of both the strengths *and the limitations* of our mental maps.

If maps were real we'd all be somewhere else!

As children we learn how to construct mental maps as a means of making sense of the bewildering array of experiences that we are going through. As we grow into adulthood, some people make as few *new* maps as they can. Some people pretend to make fresh maps, although they are really only transcribing their existing maps. And a few people make new maps all through their lives, both for the fun of it, and because they regularly seek out new experiences to learn from. There are at least three major reasons why a regular supply of new maps is desirable:

1. Maps are *always* based on a limited view of *external* reality, which is itself in a constant process of change.
2. The longer we use any particular map, the harder it becomes to recognise its shortcomings.
3. The more familiar a map becomes, the harder it is to accept the validity of anybody else's map of the same 'territory'.

Since every map is necessarily incomplete, whenever we create a new map we are forced to be selective about the information we include, a result usually arrived at by evaluating current information in the light of maps we have already prepared.

This introduces three more ways of misunderstanding external reality:

1. *Generalisation*: constructing a generally applicable rule from a very limited amount of information.
2. *Distortion*: basing our perceptions on subjective opinions rather than on objective observations.
3. *Deletion*: ignoring everything we don't like or can't be bothered with.

Some typical (twisted) workplace maps include:

- 'A tidy desk shows a tidy mind.'
  (Does a clear desk show an empty mind?)
- 'We expect our staff to behave in a professional manner.'
  (Going by the dictionary definition that simply means 'We expect that our staff will only work if they get paid for it'.)
- 'Customers don't want to be bothered with ...'
  (Who says so? Did anyone bother to ask the customers?)

CHECKPOINT ACTION

Listen to the conversations around you with the following thoughts in mind:

a. Are any generalisations, distortions or deletions being used?
b. What assumptions is each person making?
c. Are those assumptions justified?
d. What do these assumptions tell you about the speaker's mental maps?
e. What could you say to each speaker which would help them to get a better understanding of other people's points of view?

CHAPTER 3
Cultures, Values and Beliefs

Company map or virtual reality?

Strange but true, three of the most basic elements of company life – the company vision, the company mission and even company culture – are actually maps.

Unfortunately many companies devise mission statements that are decidedly short on content, as in this example taken from a brochure put out by a major examining board:

> To facilitate the best methods of flexible and effective supervisory and management education, development and assessment.

It sounds terrific, but what does it mean?

Does any reputable company deliberately set out to be *second* best? And what exactly do they mean by 'best', 'flexible' and 'effective' – all highly subjective words?

'Best' compared with whom or what? How 'flexible'? Who has defined their methods as 'effective' and how? As a map of the company's intentions, this statement is essentially meaningless. The terrain it depicts is little more than virtual reality.

All for one and ...?

We also need to understand that a business map only has

value if it embodies a *shared* reality. As one business commentator observed:

> If your company mission has to be written down and passed around, you don't have a *company* mission.

Companies which ignore this message and rely on imposed maps will, of necessity, have a punitive, autocratic culture which leaves little room for individuality. They may flourish for a while, but sooner or later they begin to crumble. The process may not become terminal if the management style can be changed in time – by re-educating the existing management or by a major reorganisation. But the changes must be genuine, or the reorganisation itself will merely speed the collapse.

No matter what the style may be, company culture is usually set by senior management and tends to change almost imperceptibly unless there is a major upheaval at this same level.

In NLP, great emphasis is placed on the need to remain true to your personal values and beliefs (see Chapter 13). If your working life seems unduly stressful, a worthwhile first step towards resolving the situation can be to review your own life maps, particularly your values and beliefs, in relation to your company's culture. On the one hand, a gradual drift into a new culture may have created a situation where you no longer share the prevailing value-set. Alternatively, the actual day-to-day running of the company may be at odds with its declared mission and vision. In either case, it may be that the simple act of identifying the mismatch is sufficient to ease the stress.

A certain American banking company sold its UK-based software house to a British company which had frequent dealings with the military establishment. Within a year, 10 of the top technicians had moved to companies where they would not be required to work on projects related to the defence industry.

A matter of choice

In that last example, the employees saw their situation as being *two-valued* – either/or. In most cases, a given situation can be viewed from *multiple* standpoints, each of which offers its own choice(s). It is a basic tenet of NLP that you don't really have a choice at all until you have at least *three* separate options to hand. Indeed, a seasoned practitioner of NLP won't even bother to count how many options they have, since the most effective response is one which changes even as the situation changes.

If you go on doing what you're doing now, you'll go on getting what you're getting now.

If you *want* something different, you have to change what you are *doing* – until you get what you want.

But what happens if you find that your personal values are at odds with those of your employer? Do you really have to hand in your resignation, or put your personal beliefs to one side while you are at work? Not at all. Just one of the alternatives is to work for promotion, in the company or in your union (if you belong to one), so as to have a greater input on company policy.

The pursuit of excellence

Nothing ever stays the same, and no business, large or small, can ever afford to rest on its laurels. In a business context, the old saying 'If it ain't broke, don't fix it' should be shunned like the plague.

Of course, there is no point in adopting change for its own sake, but any company that wants to stay ahead of the game must be constantly checking its maps against the external situation, and making appropriate adjustments when necessary.

Moreover, the process of change must be customised for

each company. Beware the consultant who offers the same handful of solutions to all of his clients. Those who espouse Japanese work styles, for example, just because they work in Japan are bound to have strictly limited success. To be of practical use, a business map must take account of local customs, culture, social parameters, and especially of changing customer needs and expectations. That which is true for Osaka is not necessarily true for Tokyo, let alone for Detroit, Manchester or Hamburg.

Trying to make a company fit a particular business theory is like altering the landscape to fit a map. Generic business theories are fine, as long as they are recognised as such and are applied at the right level. There is a point at which the application of unmodified ideas automatically becomes counterproductive.

CHECKPOINT ACTIONS

1. To what extent does the management in your company act in accordance with the declared mission/vision?
2. As briefly as possible, how would you describe the culture in each of the companies you have worked for?
3. From the list you drew up for 2, what was particularly good or bad about each culture?
4. Using the assessments you made in question 3, what could you do to improve, or encourage improvement, in the culture of your present company?
5. List the three beliefs and three values which are most important in your life, then discuss your selection with someone whose judgement you trust.

CHAPTER 4

Know What You Want to Get What You Want

What do you really want?

The results we get in life are largely self-generated. In order to succeed you must assume and believe that you are going to succeed. This goes deeper than mere 'positive thinking'.

> Whether you think you will succeed or you think you will fail, it is almost certain that you will be proved correct.

But how will you recognise success? Positive thinking, though infinitely preferable to negative thinking, is a fairly hit and miss way of achieving a desired result. Motivational speakers and pep rallies actually have a strictly limited effect. Take this example of a sales director delivering a pep talk to his 'troops':

> You are the greatest sales team it has ever been my privilege to lead. In the coming year we must be leaner and fitter, make more sales and maximise our profitability. The recession may be over but we aren't out of the woods yet.
> But we *can* do it. I *believe* we can do it. I *know* we can do it!

Like the mission statement in the last chapter, the rhetoric is stirring indeed, but what does it really mean?

What is meant by 'leaner and fitter'?

How many extra sales equal 'more'?

Does this mean that the sales people will no longer be able to offer ad hoc discounts to special customers, for example?

Has the sales director just discovered Pareto's Law (which states that approximately 80 per cent of a company's sales will be accounted for by just 20 per cent of its customers), and does he want the sales team to 'maximise profitability' by ignoring the less profitable 80 per cent of their customer base?

The audience may give the sales director a standing ovation as he finishes his speech, but will anyone actually improve their performance as a result of this emotive appeal?

Almost certainly 'no', mainly because there are no clear *outcomes* to which the sales people can respond.

The power of a well-formed outcome

Defining outcomes is a process of self-empowerment.

If I have a well-formed (clearly defined) outcome, I can make effective decisions about what I am prepared to do in order to achieve that outcome. I will also be able to assess whether, at any stage, my outcome has become impractical and must be adapted or abandoned.

Without a well-formed outcome I have little choice but simply to react to what is going on around me. Without a clear sense of direction, regardless of my status, I will be relatively ineffectual. As a result, I am likely to become increasingly frustrated, resentful and vindictive.

People respond to and work well for a person who obviously knows what they are doing, and is able to communicate positively and effectively with their superiors, colleagues and subordinates. How are you going to convince anyone that you know what you are doing, let alone motivate them to follow your lead, if your outcome(s) aren't clear in your own mind?

Your perceptions and thoughts are interactive; therefore, your current outcome will help to decide which external and internal signals you are consciously aware of.

Look, listen or feel

In order to configure effective outcomes we need first to understand the concept of *Preferred Thinking Styles* (PTSs) – the three ways in which we mentally represent the external world. The three styles are: visual, auditory and kinaesthetic: in *pictures*, by *sounds* or through *feelings* (both physical and emotional).

These PTSs tend to be related to the culture in which a person lives. In the USA, for example, the prevailing culture is highly visual, and over 50 per cent of the population have this as their PTS. In France, on the other hand, both the culture and the dominant PTS are auditory. The UK is somewhere in between, but seems to be moving towards a primarily visual culture.

People will often give verbal and non-verbal signals which indicate which PTS they are currently using. One type of non-verbal signal can be seen in people's eye movements (described in detail in Chapter 14), while the most readily recognisable verbal signal is found in the specific words chosen to convey a particular idea. These three statements all say the same thing, but each uses a markedly different choice of words:

- *Visual*: 'I don't *see* what all the fuss is about – it *looks* pretty straightforward to me.'
- *Auditory*: 'It *sounds* like a lot of fuss about nothing if you *ask* me. I'd *say* it was pretty straightforward.'
- *Kinaesthetic*: 'I don't know what people are *getting* so *upset* about. I *found* it pretty straightforward.'

Using language which reflects the other person's PTS is a key element in effective communication. If you keep using *visual* phraseology to a person whose PTS is *auditory*, for example, then you mustn't be surprised if agreement is hard to come by.

The two sample dialogues in the next box illustrate the difference between being locked into your own PTS and sharing a common vocabulary:

When PTSs Collide:

A: Have you looked at those papers I showed you?

B: I'm afraid I was tied up with other business all day.

A: You mean you didn't even glance at them?!

B: You didn't tell me they had to be dealt with in a hurry.

A: Well they do! Now, when am I going to see some action?

A 'Shared View':

C: Have you looked at those papers I showed you?

D: Not yet. You must have seen how busy I've been today.

C: So you haven't had a chance to glance through them?

D: No I haven't — but now that my desk is clear I'll give them my full attention.

C: That's great! When can I expect to see your report on my desk?

What does success look, sound and feel like?

Although each individual gives somewhat different weighting to the three PTSs, we need to take account of all three sensory modes when setting our goals in order to create an outcome which is personally meaningful.

For example, let's suppose your foremost ambition is to become wealthy. Wealth itself is relative, of course, so merely expressing your desires in a phrase such as 'I want to be wealthy' really isn't saying much at all. Is that wealthy as compared to someone living on the street, as compared to your current situation, or compared to someone who is 'financially independent' (which is another pretty vague description)?

If we turn that vague want into a 'well-formed outcome' then it becomes far more focused, and therefore far more achievable — for example:

I want to be wealthy, and I'll know that I'm wealthy when:

- I hear people around me talking about my beautiful country home, my smart clothes and my top of the range sports car.
- I see that my bank balance always exceeds £1 million.
- I feel relaxed, comfortable and unpressured at all times.

Notice that an outcome is *always* expressed in positive statements. 'I don't want to be poor' may accurately describe your viewpoint, but it leaves you facing an *undesirable* state and away from the *desired* state. 'I'll know when I am wealthy' implies a positive progression, a sequence of improvements leading to the achievement of the desired state.

In the earlier example, the sales director would almost certainly achieve more lasting results if he set some precise targets:

This time next year I want to be able to tell you that our sales for the year went over the £17 million mark. I want to see every one of you better your year-on-year figures by at least 15 per cent. I feel proud to be at the head of such a professional team.

Together we can do it. I *believe* we can do it. I *know* we can do it!

To fume, or not to fume

As we saw in Chapter 1, our emotional reactions are actually based on our *perceptions* of the events we encounter. Let's apply that knowledge to a practical situation:

Imagine that you are the production manager of a light engineering company which makes ashtrays for a leading car manufacturer. How might you react to the following events?

- You arrive at the office and the senior supervisor tells you that production in his department will stop before the end of the day shift because they are running out of lids for the ashtrays.

- The supervisor in the press shop reports reduced output because there were six absentees on the night shift, and they are also running short of metal 'blanks'.
- The stock controller says more sheet metal was ordered weeks ago, but the supplier has phoned to say that several lorry drivers are off sick and they can't deliver in less than two to three days.

So, what would *you* do?

You could get very angry, shout and curse at your own people and then phone up the suppliers and threaten to sue them for breach of contract if they don't deliver the ordered material by the end of the day. If you set this down as an outcome, it would presumably look something like this:

I want to:

- See everyone rushing around like a load of bluebottles in a jamjar, trying to make something out of nothing.
- Hear lots of excuses and arguments and the MD asking why customers aren't getting their deliveries in time.
- Feel totally frustrated and get a sore throat from shouting at everyone.

Taking control

An alternative outcome might be as follows:

I want to:

- See the production line running to schedule and goods going out of the door on time.
- Hear the supervisors telling me that everything is running smoothly, and the sales department telling me that more orders are coming in because customers are so pleased with the quality of the work and the prompt deliveries.
- Feel calm and in control. I will respond appropriately and creatively in any crisis.

The key requirement here is to get hold of some raw stock to feed the presses so that the production line can keep going. With a little thought you come up with a suitable solution. For example, you telephone your suppliers and confirm that the sheet metal is ready to be delivered. Then you call up a local haulier and arrange for a lorry to fetch the material as soon as possible. Maybe the raw materials won't arrive in time to keep the production line running until the end of the day, but it will be back on stream tomorrow. You may have to pay overtime if you need someone to unload the lorry outside normal hours. Maybe you will have to contact a staff agency to get a full quota of operators in the press shop tonight. Yet even with all these drawbacks you will still be better off than if you had simply stomped around venting your anger on everyone in sight.

CHECKPOINT ACTIONS

1. Again, listen to conversations between people at work, but this time try to detect each person's PTS.
2. Once you think that you have identified someone's PTS, see what happens if you match that PTS, and then deliberately shift into a different PTS. (Only do this with someone who won't take offence if they spot what you are doing.)
3. Is there a specific state of mind — calmness, confidence, creativity or whatever — which you would like to be able to repeat at will?

   - Think back to a time when you were in that state.
   - Take note of your feelings (emotional *and* physical), what you heard and saw, and even anything which you smelt or tasted.
   - Make your mental pictures as large, bright and focused as possible; make the sounds clear and audible, let your posture reflect what you are feeling, and so on.

     This *must* be done in an 'associated' state. (In NLP all personal experiences are identified as 'associated' (you are involved in the event), or 'dissociated' (you are watching the event as an outside observer).)
   - As the experience becomes really strong, touch yourself briefly but firmly behind your left ear lobe with your left forefinger.

- Repeat the process several times, then test the link by repeating the physical gesture while thinking about something quite different.
- Repeat the entire cycle until the physical gesture immediately calls up the positive memories. (This may take several attempts when you first try it, but you will find that the results are well worth the effort.)

CHAPTER 5
Building Relationships

The vital link

The success of *any* person-to-person communication, for *any* purpose, depends on the amount of rapport that exists between the people involved. In NLP terms, rapport is the process of creating and maintaining a harmonious relationship. With rapport there is trust and co-operation; without it there is likely to be suspicion and divisiveness. Indeed, as Sue Knight explains in her book *NLP at Work*: 'Most business decisions are made on the basis of rapport rather than technical merit'. This fact was neatly illustrated in an article in *Computing* magazine which dealt with the selection of IT training:

> As many as 91% of respondents said suppliers were selected by word of mouth, rather than a structured evaluation based on supplier presentations ...

I am not a number ...

Rapport isn't only important at the person-to-person level. As many major corporations have discovered, when a company exceeds a certain size, or is distributed over a number of separate sites, effective centralised management becomes almost impossible and internal cohesiveness begins to suffer.

Without rapport, management style becomes inflexible and bureaucratic, or fragmented and vague. In either case, the company will reflect the negative effects in its overall performance.

Unfortunately there are still plenty of companies which clearly do not understand the significance of rapport. Hence the arrival of a whole new set of jargon which, although intended to denote greater efficiency, really only serves to create greater divisiveness in the workplace. It is a basic tenet of NLP that the language we use will both reflect and shape the way we think about the world around us. Take a look at the short list of terms below and see which column *you* think is more likely to promote rapport:

A	B
HR (Human Resources)	People
HRD (Human Resource Development)	Training
O&R (Organisation and Resources)	Personnel Department

I am a free man!

NLP is about *increasing* people's effectiveness and *maximising* their potential. Moreover, in contrast with many recent developments in the business world, NLP achieves its results by fostering individuality.

BPR (Business Process Re-engineering), with its emphasis on tighter controls, down-sizing, cost-cutting exercises, and so on has done much to devalue the role of the individual. Yet despite all the hyperbole, BPR has so far failed to produce the goods. Even supporters of BPR concede that fewer than 1 per cent of corporations are fully re-engineered, and that the failure rate for BPR projects may be as high as 95 per cent!

Why? Because BPR is about theories, not people. According to James Champy, co-author of *Re-engineering the Corporation*:

> ... within the past five years we have trained a generation of managers who believe that a company is developed by reducing costs. If re-engineering only takes a cost focus, there's a high risk that it will reduce the capability and capacity of the organisation. People can't survive in companies that are shrinking.

In short, when the work environment becomes more regimented (loses rapport) so the work itself quickly loses its intrinsic value and employees become increasingly alienated. As one professional recently told me: 'work is what you do to make the money to do what you really want to do'.

Turning the tide

Rapport is the antidote to all of these negative factors. At an individual level it allows us to create more effective personal relationships, easily and quickly, even with complete strangers.

At a company level, rapport provides a basis for effective empowerment and optimal working relationships between staff and management, between departments, and so on.

Rapport can also improve customer relations – if you take the trouble to show people that you respect their beliefs and values. This does not mean that you have to share those values and beliefs, only that you acknowledge them in a positive manner.

Karen Boylston, a director at the Centre for Creative Leadership, confirms the fact that this is a key business issue:

> Customers are telling businesses, 'I don't care if every member of your staff graduated with honours from Harvard, Stanford and Wharton [top US business colleges]. I will take my business and go where I am understood and treated with respect.'

Another aspect of rapport, then, is the ability to show people that you 'understand and respect them as human beings'.

The time and the place

It is worth saying that the best relationships come about when we develop rapport *to the appropriate level*.

In a family situation it would be appropriate to develop a very deep or very warm level of rapport. In a romantic relationship the level of rapport might run to passionate or even red hot. In a business context, however, it is quite sufficient to develop rapport to the level of mutual respect.

It is also important to recognise that we may need to vary the level of rapport we have with a particular person or group, depending on the context. If we develop rapport beyond a certain level we run the danger of becoming blind to the other person's deficiencies. The 'word of mouth' selection process referred to earlier has, at its heart, a favourable assessment of the trainers/training. Awarding contracts or selecting suppliers purely on the basis of how we *feel*, rather than on the basis of an objective assessment of our business needs, is just as likely to create problems as if we had no rapport at all.

In a negotiating situation, for example, it may be beneficial to gently *break* rapport before you make an important decision. This gives you the opportunity to judge the current position on its business merits rather than simply reaching agreement because you don't want to disturb the warmth that has built up between the parties to the negotiation.

The phenomenon known as 'buyer's remorse' shows what happens when we make a decision that is overly influenced by rapport. Some salesmen understand this very well, and aim to deepen the rapport they have with the customer as they go for the close. This is fine, if it really is in the customer's interest to complete the sale. If the ploy is simply being used to make the sale there is the real danger that the customer will regret the purchase, and may come to believe that the salesman has betrayed them − which is hardly a healthy basis for any future dealings!

CHECKPOINT ACTION

In the next two chapters we will be looking at some specific techniques for developing rapport.

For the moment, you might like simply to watch how people around you relate to each other and see if you can spot any behavioural patterns which are common to:

a. Situations with a medium to high level of rapport.
b. Situations where rapport is low or even non-existent.

CHAPTER 6
Talking Body Language

Follow the leader

The first and most crucial step towards creating rapport is to *match* and *mirror* the other person's behaviour.

The technique is called matching and mirroring because the basic intent is to set yourself up as a 'mirror' for the other person by matching their behaviour, directly or indirectly, to a greater or lesser degree.

When dealing with groups you will need to match and mirror the person you are currently speaking to, while also paying attention to the person you most wish to influence.

The four mirroring techniques are:

- Mirroring *voice tone/tempo*.
- Mirroring *breathing rate*.
- Mirroring *movement*.
- Mirroring *body posture*.

These stratagems are particularly effective:

- either as a means of creating rapport when some degree of trust has already been established;
- or for deepening an existing level of rapport.

Tone and tempo

In a business context, mirroring voice tone and/or speech tempo is probably the most effective way to establish rapport.

It is relatively difficult to spot since few of us have a very accurate idea of what our voice sounds like to other people. We are even less aware of how our voices change in various situations – it depends on what we think of the person we are talking to, our current emotional state, and so on.

The *tone* of voice can be high or low, loud or soft, clear or mumbled, etc, while the *tempo* can be fast or slow, flowing or hesitant, variable or monotonous. You need only mirror the *general* characteristics of a person's voice. You need not, and should not, try to do an 'impression' of their voice, such as copying an accent, quirky mispronunciations, and so on.

No technique designed to establish rapport should ever be used in such a way that it becomes noticeable.

In general, kinaesthetics tend to speak quite slowly, often with very noticeable pauses and in a deeper than average tone. Auditory people are more likely to have even paced, well-modulated, interesting voices, while visuals often speak quite rapidly and in a higher-than-average pitch.

A breath of familiarity

Mirroring a person's *breathing rate* is a very effective way of establishing rapport, but it is also the most difficult, especially if the other person is wearing baggy clothing, keeps shifting around or, worse yet, appears to have stopped breathing.

As a rough guide, kinaesthetics usually breathe quite regularly and fully, right from the bottom of their lungs. Auditory people also breathe quite regularly, but from the mid-chest area. Visuals tend to breathe quite lightly, using only the upper chest.

If you find it difficult to spot any chest movement at all,

watch for the rise and fall of the other person's shoulders or, use a slow, shallow breathing pattern and watch for a response.

Something in the way you move

Matching *body movement* and *body posture* are the easiest forms of mirroring, but must be done with considerable discretion.

In its most literal form, I might mirror your posture, movements and gestures quite directly. If *you* lean back, then *I* will lean back; if *you* cross your legs to the left, I will cross *my* legs to the left, and so on. The only difference is that I will leave a pause before copying you, and my movements will be quite slow and subtle. The danger here is that you will detect what I am doing, at least subconsciously, and end up feeling irritation rather than rapport.

One way to avoid this error is to simulate just some of the other person's posture and gestures, leaving a varying amount of time before responding to a given movement.

Alternatively, you could use the 'cross-over mirroring' technique. Rather than directly copying the other person's actions, you make reciprocal gestures. So, if you are tapping the desk with your pencil, I might drum on my knee with my fingers *at the same tempo*. If you cross your legs, I cross my arms, and so on.

Once again, the emphasis must be on the use of smooth, discreet, apparently independent movements to avoid giving away the fact that you are actually reacting to the other person.

CHECKPOINT ACTIONS

1. Start to take conscious note of the speaking patterns of the people you talk to — tone, tempo, etc. Spend several days on this first exercise.
2. In situations where no one is likely to take offence, begin to match and mirror other people's body movements on a very limited scale.
3. Try matching other people's voice and breathing patterns, remembering that a little (done well) goes a long way.

CHAPTER 7
Follow the Leader

Walk this way

As long as you are interacting with another person, whether individually or in a group, you will be either *pacing* or *leading* that other person. That is to say, regardless of how much or how little you know about NLP, you will either:

- behave in a way that is similar to the other person's behaviour (in NLP this is called *pacing*), or
- behave in a way that is quite unlike the other person's behaviour (known as *leading*).

Successful pacing goes beyond the matching and mirroring techniques described in Chapter 6. To pace someone really effectively, you may also need to detect and mirror their beliefs, values and the content of what they say. (You don't have to share those beliefs and values in order to mirror them, of course.) Once your pacing creates a sufficient degree of rapport, you can then move on to start leading the person or people you have been pacing. Thus, you can begin to guide the customer rather than being led by him.

A graphic illustration of this switch from pacing to leading occurred when two colleagues and myself were walking back to our car in the parking lot of a motorway service station. We had gone about 40 or 50 yards, when the person in the middle suddenly pointed away to the right and asked: 'Why are we walking this way – the car's over there?'

During the relaxed conversation in the restaurant, we were effectively pacing each other. When we left the restaurant one person headed for where he *thought* that our car was located, and because of the high level of rapport between us, the other two allowed ourselves to be guided *away* from the car, even though it was in full view throughout the incident.

Leading to win

In a business situation, once a significant degree of rapport has been established by matching the other person's behaviour, the pacer should be able to transfer smoothly into leading mode in order to bring the event to its desired conclusion.

But beware. Pacing and leading are only truly effective when both leader *and* those being led are headed towards a win-win situation. A 'leader' who works towards a win-lose conclusion (ie where she wins and they lose) is quite likely to find that the whole manoeuvre falls apart as the 'victims' wake up to the true nature, and consequences, of the transaction.

CHECKPOINT ACTIONS

1. Watch how pacing and leading occur in workplace interactions. Is it always the more senior person who does the leading?
2. Use body movements and voice to create rapport, then see what changes you need to make in order to:

   a. Lead the other person.
   b. Break rapport.

CHAPTER 8
Give the Dog a New Name

Anchors aweigh!

If you completed the third Checkpoint Action for Chapter 4, you will remember how you were able to recall a positive frame of mind by using a simple physical gesture. In NLP this process of creating a mental link between an internal feeling and an external event is known as anchoring. As you have already discovered, an anchor is a learned response, which means that we can create, alter and dissolve anchors, at will, in order to achieve specific results.

The higher the fewer

Unfortunately, we often create these anchors in everyday life. For example, in many companies today, the higher you go up the management ladder, the fewer people you will find who have any great length of service in that company.

It is as though companies have such a negative view of the link between loyalty and competence that the only way to get promoted is to leave.

Why do companies act in this way? At first sight, such behaviour may seem somewhat self-defeating, yet it does prove to make sense if we relate it to the NLP concept of anchoring.

Just as a particular feeling can be anchored to a particular piece of music, so our feelings about a particular person can become anchored to a specific situation, such as seeing that person in the same role day after day, month after month.

When this kind of anchoring occurs, when we label someone by their job title (or their sex, or their skin colour), instead of seeing them as a unique individual, they can become anchored (in our thoughts) to a particular response. Once this happens, it can take something like a resignation before we can clear the anchors and recognise that person's true worth.

Companies with a clear pattern of 'promotion through resignation' need to look very closely at the company culture. Some training in basic people skills may be long overdue.

The same problem exists when we characterise a person by judgemental labels ('maverick', 'loner', etc.), as though the person and their behaviour are the same thing. That is to say, when we 'give a dog a bad name'.

Put very simply, we tend to see what we *expect* to see, so when we give someone a label we severely limit our own ability to take an objective view of that person. Moreover, while people cannot change what they 'are', we can change our *behaviour* in any way we want, whenever we want. The biggest barrier to change is usually not in the individual, but in other people's refusal to accept that change might be possible.

Inadvertent hypnosis

There is now substantial evidence that we all tend to drift in and out of a 'trance state' on a regular basis throughout our waking hours. During these incidents, which occur every 90 minutes and last for some 15–20 minutes (both timings are approximate), we may find that we are clumsier, more easily distracted and more suggestible. (These trances seem to be an intuitive way of taking time to process incoming information.)

The discovery of these trance episodes illustrates our ability to enter 'altered states of consciousness' in a very easy and natural manner. This in turn helps to explain the phenomenon known as 'inadvertent hypnosis'.

Suppose, for a moment, that you have the job of helping someone learn to ride a bike. Would you tell them:

- 'Keep it steady', or
- 'Don't let it wobble'?

The difference between these two phrases may seem trivial in the extreme, yet in the real world the first instruction will be heard as a positive and supportive command, while the second is an invitation to disaster. The point to note here is that the human brain often *cannot* hear exactly what is being said.

Don't think about a blue elephant

Okay, are you *not* thinking about a blue elephant? Of course you aren't. It just isn't possible to know whether you are *not* thinking about something unless you think about that thing in order to know what it is you're not going to think about!

In short, the human brain simply cannot think in negatives. If I say 'Keep it steady', the trainee can choose to do precisely that. But if I say 'Don't let it wobble', then they must first think about wobbling in order to know what it is they shouldn't do. The conscious mind hears the message as spoken: 'Don't wobble', but the subconscious mind (which controls our response) hears a very different message: 'Wobble – don't'. And by the time it hears 'don't' it may already have heard, and carried out, the perceived command to wobble out of control!

CHECKPOINT ACTIONS

1. As you meet with friends and colleagues, be aware of the extent to which your reactions are based on past events. Are you really seeing people as they are *now*, or as they used to be?
2. When decisions have to be made, to what extent do you choose to do things 'the way we've always done them'? Are you losing out on efficiency and creativity by refusing to accept the need for and likely benefits of change?

CHAPTER 9

When You Put It Like That ...

It's the way you tell 'em

Two people say almost exactly the same thing, yet one version sounds like a threat and one is a simple comment.

Why? Because everything that happens, happens 'in context'.

When someone speaks to us we take account of who they are, what we think about them, and so on. If a friend telephones and says 'Have you got a minute?' in a cheery tone of voice, that will carry a totally different connotation than if your boss suddenly ambushes you as you pass his office and asks in a sombre tone 'Have you got a minute?'

> The meaning of what you say is the response that it gets.

In NLP jargon, everything we say and do occurs within what is referred to as a 'frame'. We've all been in a situation when, for no apparent reason, people have responded to us in a way that was totally at odds with our intentions. It's as though they were responding to the frame instead of to the picture.

What will they hear when you speak?

Very simply, an effective frame is a way of presenting your message so as to increase the chance that people will hear what you *mean*, not just what you *say*. Understanding the importance of the frame will enable you to choose how to present a request, statement or order so as to give it maximum effect. For example:

> It isn't easy for me to say this, because I know it may sound unpleasant, and it may seem as though I haven't given you credit for all the hard work that you've put into preparing this presentation. It is my job to make sure that we show ourselves to our customers in the best possible light. For that reason alone I'm going to ask you to go back and rework this presentation.
>
> It needs to be shorter and punchier – not more than 40 to 45 minutes, maximum – and I want you to replace the jargon with language that the customer will understand.
>
> Is that clear?

This explanation shows that you've thought about how your comments will be received, without being falsely apologetic. It also gives a credible reason for being critical rather than simply saying 'This presentation is useless – go and do it again!'

The third section – 'It needs ...' – offers some constructive guidelines for improvement, and again shows that you've given the matter some thought rather than just reacting against something you didn't like.

Lastly, 'Is that clear?' is ambiguous enough to be answered yes or no, or to open the way for more discussion, if necessary.

Requests can also benefit by being well framed. In particular, the *reason* for the request should always precede the request:

> I don't know if you're aware of this fact – a recent study showed that it takes a typist up to two hours to produce a simple letter. And even then the result often leaves a lot to be desired.
>
> These new word-processing machines can check spelling and grammar, and you don't have to rewrite a whole document just because you want to take something out, add something or

switch a few sentences around. These things can pay for themselves in next to no time.

That's why I'm suggesting that we replace all the machines in the typing pool with word processors.

Apart from a hint of a request at the start of the second paragraph, it is only after some very relevant advantages have been described that we finally find out what the speaker is actually asking for. The listener cannot reasonably answer the request until it has been clearly specified − in the final sentence!

But suppose the speaker had started out in reverse order:

I'm putting in this request to replace all the typewriters in the typing pool with word processors.

I don't know if you're aware of this fact − a recent study showed that it takes a typist ...

This way round the listener can make a decision immediately, and totally ignore the explanation, no matter how good.

Sweetening the pill

About 70–80 per cent of the population tend to be resistant to change, to a greater or lesser extent. This means that the way in which news of a change is presented is often crucial to successful implementation of that change. Here again, framing can make the difference between success and failure.

When introducing new technology, for example, salesmen and enthusiasts tend to use phrases like:

- 'It's a whole *new way* of working'
- 'This will *revolutionise* working practices'
- 'These are the machines *of the future*'

Imagine how these phrases must sound to someone who is averse to change. No wonder so many people, including many managers, show signs of technophobia.

How much easier would it be if the new technology was introduced within a more sensitive frame, such as:

- A way to make your job *easier*.
- In most respects, as *straightforward* as using a typewriter.
- *Full training* will be provided.

By changing the phrasing, the changes become *evolutionary* rather than *revolutionary*, and much less threatening.

On the other hand . . .

Where framing *creates* a context, reframing *reshapes* the context. It is a way of reviewing an existing situation or idea so that the content can be re-evaluated. It can be used to give a broader view of a business decision, or to gain greater understanding of someone else's 'map' of a particular occurrence.

Long-termism versus short-termism in business is just one example of how reframing has become a badly needed skill.

In the world of computer programming, for instance, there has been a trend towards:

- Shedding permanent staff.
- Making increasing use of contract labour.

In the short term, this has at least two important advantages:

- Contractors need only be employed as long as there is work for them to do.
- Specialist skills can be bought in when needed rather than paying for regular staff to be trained up.

If we reframe the action, however, we see that there are limitations as well as advantages:

- Contractors don't have the same loyalty or self-interest in the success of the company as do permanent staff members.
- If your systems have been developed by a group of people who have all moved on, who is there in-house who really understands what it's all about?

The initial frame seemed very attractive, and was correct, as far as it went. Only by reframing the possible outcomes can we appreciate both the advantages and the drawbacks of each alternative, decide whether the action is still worth taking, and, if it is, how we can minimise any negative side effects.

Trouble is a state of mind

At a personal level we may adopt another viewpoint in order to broaden our own understanding, or we may feed someone else's viewpoint back to them in such a way that they can appreciate some additional information which they had not previously considered.

One of the most important reframes needed in many companies today concerns customer relationships. How often do you hear the complaint that customers expect everything, preferably yesterday, and for free. It's true that most customers can be difficult from time to time, but how much business can you do without any customers?

The reframe on this point is simply this: if all customers can be difficult at one time or another, then having difficulties with customers is an integral part of running a successful business. Difficult customers aren't really a burden at all – they are proof of success!

CHECKPOINT ACTIONS

1. You have to ask someone to re-do a task when there really isn't any excuse for not having done it properly the first time round.

   - How would you frame your comments to get a positive response?
   - How do you feel about trying to be positive when the other person is so clearly at fault?

   Repeat this exercise with several different work colleagues in mind. Is there a difference depending on the person you have in mind? If so, why?

---

2. Make it a habit, whenever you hear a negative comment, to look for a striking reframe. For example:

Comment: 'I hate getting up at 7am every morning!'
Reframe: 'You wouldn't have that problem if you didn't have a job.'

Do this in response to your own negative thoughts.

CHAPTER 10

Clear Thinking or Gut Feeling?

Hot buttons

As advertising agency people are well aware, we all have 'hot buttons' which, when pressed, may cause us to attach greater importance to our 'gut feelings' than to our rational thoughts, and to act accordingly. That's why gooey love stories and lurid melodramas may bring us close to tears even when, intellectually, we know that what we are watching is pure fiction.

In NLP these hot buttons are called *meta programs* – the deepest of the unconscious filters involved when we perceive, and respond to, the world around us.

Perceptions, thoughts and emotions

In order to appreciate the role of meta programs it is essential that we understand the relationship between perceptions, thoughts and emotions. For example, if our perceptions shape our emotions, what shapes our perceptions?

We now know that our perceptions are filtered and re-evaluated according to our previous experiences, beliefs, values and knowledge.

If we can recognise which filters people are using, we can

anticipate how they are likely to react to what we do and say.

Only thinking makes it so

In his play of the same name, Shakespeare gives Hamlet the words: 'There is nothing either good or bad, but thinking makes it so'. This is certainly true of meta programs, which have no ethical content at all. They are simply programs or thought processes which we use to filter incoming information.

One of the key meta programs linked to motivation, for example, indicates the specific words which are most likely to encourage or deter a person in relation to some plan of action. These 'modal operators' are pairs of words such as: 'must and mustn't', 'should and shouldn't', and so on. These are the words a person says inside their head when deciding on a course of action: 'I *must* leave home on time to get the 8:45 train', 'I *shouldn't* eat any more chocolates', and so on.

The logic behind the use of these words may sometimes be totally flawed, yet that is not enough, in itself, to break their power. Indeed, the self-same words may be used by some people to *avoid* taking the very action that they seem to support. The best known example of this phenomenon is the expression: 'I really must try to' which almost always means, in practice: 'I'll think about it, but that's as far as I go'.

In Chapter 18 we will look at seven of the most frequently encountered meta programs, plus the modal operators.

CHECKPOINT ACTIONS

1. Start looking out for the use of modal operators, both by other people and in your own speech, phrases like:
   'I can/can't', 'I must/mustn't', 'I ought to ...', 'I should ...', and so on.
2. See how often you apply these operators to other people:
   'They ought to ...', 'He shouldn't do that!', and so on
   How does this affect the way that you react to those people?

CHAPTER 11

Making Information Make Sense

Bottom lines and aerial views

You may want to answer the following questions before you read on. It will make the practical application of the information in this chapter much easier to understand.

Q1. When learning about something new, do you prefer to (A) start with an overview and work down to specific details, or (B) build up to the overall view, detail by detail?

If you chose option A, then answer Q2, otherwise answer Q3.

Q2. Are you really interested in detailed information, or would you prefer to stick with the overview?

Q3. Are you really interested in the 'big picture', or would you prefer to stick with the details?

Q1	Q2	Q3	Chunk type
A	No	–	Abstract
A	Yes	–	Abstract to specific
B	–	No	Specific
B	–	Yes	Specific to abstract

Up the down staircase

A key element in Alfred Korzybski's *General Semantics* (see Chapter 1) was what he called the 'ladder of abstraction'. One of the main reasons why we fail to communicate effectively, Korzybski said, was because we so often use *vague* language, and expect other people to understand *precisely* what we mean.

Sometimes this isn't particularly important. If I say that I'm going to London next week, by train, it really doesn't matter whether you understand that I plan to travel first class on the 8:43am Intercity Express from King's Sittingbourne next Friday and will return the same day, or you just think 'London, by train'. But suppose that I want to buy a ticket for that journey, and you are the ticket clerk. In that case, it matters a great deal whether you understand exactly what I've planned, because the precise combination of these details will determine what kind of ticket I get and how much it will cost.

The NLP label for the process of moving up or down the ladder of abstraction is *stepping* or, more usually, *chunking*. When we chunk *up* we start with the details ('specifics') and work up to the overview. Chunking *down* means breaking down an 'abstract' overview into ever more precise details.

In a business context, people who prefer to deal in specifics tend to be 'backroom boys'. They seldom rise very high on the management scale because they don't feel comfortable dealing with anything that seems vague or imprecise.

Those who rise highest on the corporate ladder, even though they may have started out acquiring specific skills, usually have the ability to take in, and make decisions from, the 'big picture', without worrying too much about the 'nitty-gritty' details.

Plus or minus two

According to one famous study, human beings can only consciously deal with seven 'chunks' of information, plus or minus two, at any given moment. But just how much information is there in a 'chunk'?

The simple answer is that there is no simple answer. Chunk size varies from person to person, and even from topic to topic. It also tends to grow in size as you become more familiar with the material. Just consider the following 'explanation':

> For VAT purposes, cross debit incomings and outgoings and enter the transaction in the day book and the residue in the bought ledger, unless the rolling annual total becomes negative, in which case record the transaction as an inverse credit payment, and enter the balance on an F11/789/K.

To the average person this paragraph contains at least 8 chunks of information and probably looks quite genuine. An experienced bookkeeper, however, will probably see at a glance that the whole thing is sheer nonsense.

Picking the right level

Selecting the correct chunk size in a given situation, and knowing whether to chunk up or down – or both – are key skills in interpersonal communication.

No matter what the situation, if you chunk correctly you have a significantly better chance of getting your message across. Choose the wrong chunk size, or chunk in the wrong direction and you might as well stay at home.

Abstract people
These people just want to see the big picture. Get too detailed and the Abstract listener begins to switch off. If you really *must* go into details, then keep them as few and as simple as possible, and make sure that you present them in an interesting or amusing way.

Abstract to specific people
This group needs the overview first in order to have a framework on which to hang the details which follow. Although they are willing to deal with a certain amount of detail, they have an instinctive feel (not necessarily infallible)

for how much detail they need about a given subject. Once you cross this boundary – if you start to get *too* specific – then they are also likely to simply tune you out.

Specific people

'But I did exactly what you asked. How was I to know the information was for a customer?' is typical of the sort of complaint made by the Specific person. They may be excellent at their particular job, but will find it difficult to relate what they do to the business of the department or company as a whole.

When taking on new information/skills, Specific people like to have plenty of details, preferably with the underlying theory and some basic hands-on experience. Indeed, some Specifics never feel ready to actually use a new skill until their knowledge is positively encyclopedic.

Specific to abstract people

This is the most practical of the four groups we have looked at. They do need to get some detailed information in front of them when they approach a new activity, learn a new skill or whatever, but at least they are willing to build on that information to work towards a synergistic understanding (that is, a view that is greater than the mere sum of the details).

People in this group are often seen as the backbone of a company. They're happy to do what they do day in and day out with commendable consistency, yet are capable of flashes of unexpected creativity given expert management or even just because a set of details suddenly falls into place.

CHECKPOINT ACTIONS

1. Select a topic on a subject you know well.
2. Imagine that you are going to discuss this topic with two groups of people:
   - Group A are familiar with the subject but not the topic.
   - Group B have no background knowledge on the subject or this specific topic.
3. Break down the topic into 'chunks' suitable for each group and decide, in each case, whether you need to chunk up or to chunk down for the best effect.

CHAPTER 12
Avoiding Resistance

I wanna tell you a story

A certain man, an architect by profession, was asked by a friend to draw up plans for a modest town house.

'I've bought some land, and though I have no experience, I'm sure it can't be hard to build your own house. After all, if it were hard, there wouldn't be so many of them, would there?'

The architect, realising that his friend would not allow himself to be argued out of his intention, worked on the plans as requested, taking special care to make them as comprehensive and as easy to follow as he possibly could.

About two weeks later the architect went down to the site to see how things were getting on. He was amazed to find his friend standing beside a large stack of new bricks, with a mound of broken bricks on his other side.

He was even more amazed to see his friend take a brick from the pile on his left and hit it with a hammer, then toss the pieces on to the mound of broken bricks on his right.

'What on earth are you doing?' asked the architect, 'you're destroying perfectly good bricks treating them like that.'

'Perfectly good bricks?' said the friend, 'I don't think so. See how easily they break. The bricks with which I build my house will have to support a structure that weighs tons. I need to know whether the materials are good enough to do the job!'

The heart of the matter

Pierre Casse, a professor at the International Institute for Management Development in Lausanne says, regarding the use of metaphors: 'When you hear a negotiator say, *'Oh, that reminds me of a story ...'* – **be alert** – **at once** ... **a story** is always dangerous in the sense that it is a **metaphor** ...' (italics and bold highlighting as in the original text).

A metaphor, as Professor Casse explains, works on at least two levels. On the conscious level, it is simply what it appears to be – an anecdote or fable. On the second level, it allows us to talk to the subconscious mind in such a way that the conscious mind cannot censor or reject the underlying message(s).

In the story at the start of this chapter, for example, the overt message is a mild kind of joke.

At the deeper level, the story has several messages, including:

- Even an expert can't necessarily prevent a friend from making a fool of himself.
- Don't assume that a job is easy just because it's been done many times before.
- Logic becomes counter-productive when applied in an illogical manner.

One word of warning before we move on: because metaphors always carry indirect messages, anyone who hears the story, even if it was not meant for them, may hear a deeper meaning which you, the story teller, had never thought of or intended.

CHECKPOINT ACTIONS

1. Watch how frequently people explain themselves with little stories. How does this affect your own understanding of what (you think) they are trying to say?
2. Use story-telling to enliven your own conversation.
   (But remember, in the business context, *short* stories work best – see Chapter 19.)

CHAPTER 13
Self-Management

Do you mean what you say?

It may be hard to comprehend just how little effect what we *say* may have if it does not convey the same message given out by our vocal characteristics (tone, tempo, variability, etc) and our body language. If these three factors are not in accord — if we are not *congruent* — people will weigh up the message that they receive from each of the three forms of communication:

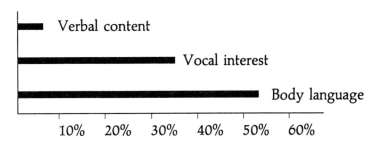

These figures show why we need to understand and manage our own *non-verbal* cues if we want our message to be heard.

Values and beliefs

True congruence only occurs when we are behaving in complete accordance with our beliefs and values, when we are working to a clear-cut and well-focused outcome, and when our words, vocal signals and body language are naturally synchronised.

Admittedly, much of life consists of making compromises, and achieving complete congruence is something of a struggle.

One way of achieving congruence is to push everything else to one side. Like a top-class athlete we can become so focused on the job in hand that nothing else intrudes upon our thoughts to distract us from achieving a particular outcome.

This is, however, a strategy with definite limitations. Applied for short periods it can be extremely effective, but if we make this our primary behaviour pattern over a protracted period, we are likely to become, in other people's view, not congruent but 'obsessive', 'blinkered' and afflicted with 'tunnel vision'.

True congruence is a source of tremendous sustainable power in the context of achieving outcomes. It is a way of being highly focused without becoming cold, ruthless or any of the other negative qualities we normally associate with an out-and-out go-getter. This is achieved by maintaining, as far as possible, an integrated posture by getting all of your parts to act in harmony.

A typical example of *incongruence* in the workplace is the person who values the social perks of belonging to a team, but who also wants to be recognised for their efforts as an individual. An adept team leader or manager will ensure that his people get an adequate supply of personal recognition without having to act in a way which could disrupt the smooth running of the team.

The sum of the parts

Have you ever said something like: 'I think I agree, but part of me still isn't convinced'? According to NLP, when you talk this way — 'part of me', 'I'm a *bit* worried', 'I'm *not entirely* sure' — it is something more than a mere figure of speech.

The 'bit' or 'part' is some portion of your subconscious which carries out a particular action or otherwise serves (or has served) some useful purpose. A typical 'part' is the 'little critic', the internal voice that serves a useful purpose by guiding us away from making careless mistakes, but which can also eat away at our self-confidence if it is constantly carping.

These parts are what we deal with in the *programming* aspect of NLP, and getting all of your parts to work together is the basis of a congruent posture. The more unanimity there is between the parts – the more congruent you are – the greater the potential for effective action.

Talking to parts

Imagine what it might be like to have a fear of heights. One part of you might say: 'I want to go to the fifteenth floor of this building to attend an important meeting', but if another part says: 'No way, that's much too high – I'm not going up there!', there is a distinct chance that you won't get to the meeting.

To achieve congruence you might do a deal with the part that is afraid of heights, such as: 'I'll go to the fifteenth floor but I won't watch the floor indicator in the lift, I won't look out of the windows, and I'll come back down as soon as I can.'

This is not to say that it is necessary to believe that your *self* is divided literally into hundreds of separate 'parts'. Like much of NLP, the concept of parts is simply a metaphor designed to convey an idea which works *as if* it were literally true.

It is possible, however, to have conversations with your parts, as the fear of heights example suggested, and this can be very effective in a range of business situations.

The essential point is to recognise that the tensions that arise within us when we approach an important, new or emotionally charged experience (or any other experience, for that matter) are perfectly natural. The real question is: will we try to struggle through without resolving the tension, in a state of *in*congruence, or will we reprogram our response to achieve a more harmonious, congruent and effective state?

Andrew Carnegie, self-made multi-millionaire and philanthropist, would often break off in the middle of a business meeting and go into another office by himself while he talked through the progress of the meeting. Only when he had clarified his own position – his own outcome – would he rejoin the meeting.

Never negotiate with yourself in front of your competitors.

Incidentally, we usually recognise significant states of congruence or incongruence in other people, and vice versa. The phrase: 'I don't know why, he just made me feel uncomfortable' is a typical expression of this instinctive awareness.

'Need-to-know' management

A congruence-related situation which has a significant effect on staff performance in some companies is the practice of 'need-to-know'-style management: 'If you need to know, I'll tell you; if I don't tell you, then you don't need to know.'

Companies which support this practice would presumably argue that it is the right of management to release information 'at their own discretion'. But if it is impossible to know *everything* about even the most simple situation, how can we ever know in advance what people will *need to know*?

In practice, this authoritarian approach tends to create wholly unnecessary tensions, and invariably sabotages the very efficiency it is supposed to foster. Companies are much more likely to succeed by promoting mutually respectful staff/management relations, treating staff like responsible adults.

CHECKPOINT ACTION

We all talk to our parts at some time or other, and these internal dialogues are perfectly natural. So get into the habit of listening to your inner voice. Learn to take advantage of your 'hidden depths', and take control of the 'little critic'.

CHAPTER 14
Using Preferred Thinking Styles

The medium is the message

In the process of filtering our experiences, according to one or more Preferred Thinking Styles (PTSs), we also create a highly personalised view of the world (Chapter 2).

We are usually wholly unaware that this process is taking place, yet it has tremendous influence in our lives. When a conversation between two people is based on different PTSs (Chapter 4), they might as well be talking different languages. Each can hear what the other person is *saying*, yet they find it almost impossible to understand what the other person *means*.

Imagine for a moment that your own PTS is auditory – sound. You visit a car showroom and the salesman goes on and on about the incredible *design* of the car, and the *feel* of the hide upholstery. His description may be quite true, but it is virtually meaningless in terms of making the sale.

But what happens if the salesman demonstrates the almost inaudible 'click' as the door shuts? Or the powerful throb as the engine revs up and then drops to a gentle murmur?

Please note that these are not meant to be 'in depth' character studies. Their accuracy, in regard to any specific person, will depend on such factors as: How dominant is the main PTS and in what order are the other two PTSs rated? (eg a*Visual* may be VAK (Visual/Auditory/Kinesthetic) or VKA (Visual/Kinesthetic/Auditory)).

Look sharp!

An estimated 50–55 per cent of the business population is made up of people whose PTS is Visual. Visuals code their experiences in graphical form and therefore respond most readily to incoming information which is already coded in a visual format. Visuals can be recognised by their use of vision-oriented language:

'I see what you mean.'
'Looks good to me.'
'Show me more.'

and by their eye movements. Visuals tend to look upwards or straight ahead when thinking:

Visual imagine   Visualisation   Visual recall

Typical Visuals will think, talk and behave as though their entire mental processes are held on film. They tend to be relatively fast talkers, and may be impatient when interrupted because they need to talk as fast as the film show running in their heads. Interruptions may mean that they literally 'lose part of the picture'. At best, they may be able to rerun the film and pick up at the point where they were interrupted. At worst, that part of their thoughts may be lost entirely.

Visuals often use their hands quite freely in a way that complements whatever they are saying. In fact, they tend to move around a lot in general, pacing the floor while talking and looking around at anything other than the person they are speaking to. This may be irritating for non-Visuals, but it certainly does not signal a lack of respect or interest. On the contrary, Visuals behave this way to avoid anything which might distract them from that internal film show.

The main advantages of the visual PTS are the ability to 'see' the big picture, yet just as easily to zoom in on a specific detail ('cutting to the bottom line', as they might put it). Visuals also tend to be better at 'thinking on their feet' than Auditories or Kinaesthetics.

Their main disadvantages are an over-dependence on visual information, low tolerance when interrupted, and difficulty in dealing with any kind of information which cannot readily be represented in graphical form.

Visual managers

When you hear a manager saying something like 'It's not what you do, it's what you look like you're doing', or 'It's people's perceptions that count', you can be certain that you're listening to someone whose PTS is visual. The problem is, of course, that you can't *see* someone thinking. This means that a visual manager may easily fall into the trap of assuming that the person who is always hustling round with a fist full of papers is doing more work than someone who is relatively static because whatever task they're engaged in takes a great deal of thought.

Taken to extremes, a visual manager can so demotivate the people doing the real work that he ends up with a department full of paper shufflers, yet believes that he has successfully swept the department clean of time wasters!

Visual managers might want to take a little more notice of who actually produces results, as distinct from who simply *looks* busy. And is it really only perceptions which count? Not if you want to hang on to your best staff. Remember, we normally see what we choose to see and what we expect to see. Are you looking out for the best interests of the company, or judging things from a purely personal point of view?

If you work for a visual boss, find ways of showing her what you have achieved. Don't waste time *telling* your boss what you've been doing; if you can't back up your words with something visual, it will go in one ear and out the other.

Visual employees

If you're thinking of employing someone with a visual PTS make sure that they will be a long way away from anything to do with customer relations. Their real talents lie in areas that demand visual skills – designer, architect, photographer, and so on.

Auditories

Is there anyone in your company who habitually talks to themself, especially when they are concentrating really hard? In all likelihood they have a strong auditory PTS.

As the name implies, Auditories interact with the world around them primarily through sounds, and especially through words. An Auditory will typically use expressions like:

> 'I hear what you say.'
> 'Sounds good to me.'
> 'Tell me more.'

The Auditory eye movements are to left and right, at eye level, except when they are mentally rehearsing what they wish to say or deciding what they ought to say (internal dialogue):

Audio imagine   Internal dialogue   Audio recall

Although they make up only 20–30 per cent of the workforce, Auditories play an important part in the life of the companies they work for. If you want someone who really will perform well in a customer-facing function, be sure to put 'auditory PTS' at the top of your list of required qualifications.

Like human 'voice analysers', Auditories are very aware of the 'non-verbal' messages we give out when we are speaking (although they may not realise that they have this skill).

The main drawback for Auditories is that they have a particularly strong need for a quiet or soothing background as they are easily distracted by loud or disharmonious noises. (It has been shown that creating an auditorially soothing background in the workplace can reduce absenteeism and raise productivity by as much 18 and 22 per cent respectively.) For this reason many Auditories prefer to get to work early or stay on late, in order to have some time when they can work without being disturbed.

Some Auditories may tend to be somewhat assertive, even domineering, in meetings and even in simple conversations. This is because Auditories often need to verbalise their thoughts in order to clarify their own ideas.

By the same token, Auditories respond best to instructions and information which is delivered primarily in words, at a tempo roughly equivalent to their own normal rate of speech, and by someone with an interesting voice. They are more likely to ask questions and come back for verbal clarification after a presentation or after having been assigned a task. This is simply because Auditories find written handouts and instructions less meaningful and convincing than straight verbal communication.

Having said that, Auditories are the one group who actually benefit from a 'need-to-know' policy (Chapter 13). Unlike Visuals and Kinaesthetics, who can store information in hard copy format (and review it at their leisure), Auditories make their decisions very largely on the basis of what they *hear*, or more precisely, on what they can *remember* of what they have heard. Thus Auditories usually dislike being offered multiple options (in a training situation, for example) and often find it relatively difficult to come down on one side or another in an argument or discussion.

Auditory managers
When dealing with an Auditory boss, the best course is to present your information or request as succinctly as possible, in verbal form, then to leave him to make a decision.

Use a vocal style that is varied and interesting, remembering that Auditories often think in a dialogue mode. Where relevant, ask questions which will direct that dialogue in the appropriate direction (use questions that begin with 'What?' not 'Why?').

When taking instructions from an Auditory manager, remember that they may not know exactly what they want you to do until they hear themselves say it out loud. Be prepared for an Auditory to run through the details more than once as they sort things out in their own mind, and leave your comments or questions until they have clearly finished their message.

Auditory employees

Visual and Kinaesthetic managers need to remember that Auditories are usually quick on the uptake, but need to make sense of whatever is said to them before they can act on it. A memo may seem like a good idea to you, but a short conversation will be far more effective in the long run. Encourage them to ask (relevant) questions and give (constructive) feedback wherever you can.

Kinaesthetics

Like Auditories, the people who have kinaesthetic as their PTS make up approximately one-quarter of the working population. The word 'kinaesthetic' comes from the Greek words *kinein* (to move) and *aisthesthai* (to perceive), and is therefore most commonly used to refer to the physical sense of movement. In NLP the word is used to refer to 'feelings' in general, both physical and emotional. This is reflected in Kinaesthetics' style of speech, which tends to be a little slower than average (as they make frequent internal checks on their feelings), and in their use of expressions such as:

> 'I get what you're saying.'
> 'I feel good about that.'
> 'Fill me in on the details.'

Only one form of kinaesthetic eye movement has been

identified at this time – down and to the left (as seen by an observer):

Sensory recall

More than any other group, Kinaesthetics attach great importance to their feelings (especially their emotions). Unfortunately, emotions have no content, as such, and also tend to be somewhat transitory. Thus Kinaesthetics often find it difficult to deal with logical reasoning until they have decided how they *feel* about the topic in question.

Internal Kinaesthetics are primarily attuned to their own feelings and can appear to be rather introverted and insensitive, even 'cold'. External Kinaesthetics, on the other hand, are much more attuned to the people and events around them. They are likely to feel particularly unsettled and vulnerable in an emotionally charged or physically chaotic situation. (The words 'internal' and 'external' are used here in reference to the relevant meta program – see Chapter 18.)

Kinaesthetics may have trouble dealing with high-pressure situations, as they need time to interpret incoming information in relation to previous experiences and emotions. Having said that, Kinaesthetics who have learned to balance the internal and external aspects of their PTS often achieve considerable success in business, especially in areas which demand a high degree of empathy, such as negotiating and personnel functions.

Kinaesthetic managers
Kinaesthetic managers place little importance on the kind of information that appeals to Visuals and Auditories, preferring to rely on their 'gut reactions'. This can lead to notable successes, or equally notable fiascos when they miss the mark.

Having reached a decision, Kinaesthetic managers will find it difficult to change their minds, even when contrary evidence is placed before them. In order to deliver your message convincingly to a Kinaesthetic, you will need to reach her at an emotional level, a task which is most easily achieved through the use of metaphors (Chapter 12). Unfortunately there is no guarantee that your Kinaesthetic listener will receive the message that you intended.

Kinaesthetic employees

Employees who have a Kinaesthetic PTS may require considerable patience, since they will tend to prioritise their work according to their personal feelings about each task. It pays, then, to give each job emotional weighting as it is assigned – for example, 'I'd really appreciate it if you'd give this matter top priority', or 'I'm not too worried when you do this as long as it's ready by the end of the week'.

It is also important to note that Kinaesthetics need an emotional framework in everything that they do. This includes building internal versions of the feelings of the people they work with, which they then interpret as fact. The middle ranking manager who seems to understand senior management's innermost thoughts, and insists that everyone behaves according to this 'knowledge', is a typical kinaesthetic 'mind reader'.

CHAPTER 15
Presentations

Who are you talking to?

Presentations come in all shapes and sizes, from a one-to-one training session up to a major bells and whistles and coloured lights media event. Obviously, the way you handle a particular presentation should reflect the size and purpose of the event.

We have picked out five elements which are applicable to *any* presentation, which form the rather appropriate mnemonic OSCAR:

clear	**Outcome**
layered	**Structure**
selective	**Chunking**
positive	**Attitude**
flexible	**Response**

Outcome

No presentation is going to be successful if it doesn't have a clearly defined outcome or set of outcomes. (Chapter 4).

The outcome(s) of a presentation should be clearly detailed at the start of the event and adhered to. This provides a framework which will make it easier for your audience to understand and remember the points made during the presentation.

Structure

In order to effectively utilise Preferred Thinking Styles (Chapters 4 and 14) and meta programs (Chapters 10 and 18), take extra care over the structure of your presentation. Make sure that you switch frequently, but not obviously, from one PTS to another throughout the presentation, and cater to any meta programs you think appropriate (Towards – Away, Sameness – Difference, etc).

Chunking

Also on the subject of meta programs, be sure to 'chunk' your material (Chapter 11) so as to retain audience interest.

Since individual members of your audience will have different preferences, your best option is to choose a middle-of-the-range starting point and then chunk up. Allow questions from the audience so that people can ask for more detail if they wish, but avoid getting bogged down in 'nitty-gritty' details (unless that level of detail is a necessary element of the event).

Attitude

This means more than simply 'think positive'. Effective presenters share an unusually high level of self-confidence, at least while they are giving a presentation. It is as though they will the event to succeed by their unflagging belief in that success, a belief that will be conveyed to and impressed upon the audience through a variety of non-verbal signals.

Response

There are at least three viewpoints in any situation: your own, the other person's, and that of an impartial observer.

The fifth quality that contributes to a truly impressive presentation style is a mixture of sensitivity and flexibility. Top presenters constantly switch back and forth between viewpoints, always aware of the response they are getting from their audience, and able to customise the presentation as they go in order to achieve their desired outcome.

CHAPTER 16
Discipline

X, Y and NLP

According to Douglas McGregor, there are two basic styles of management:

Theory X
Managers who adopt Theory X do so on the assumption that:

- Employees are naturally lazy, irresponsible and none too bright.
- It is management's task to direct, motivate and control employees according to the needs of the organisation.

Theory Y
Managers following the Theory Y scenario assume that:

- Employees already have motivation, a readiness to accept responsibility and the potential for self-development.
- It is management's task to make it possible for people to achieve their own goals *best* by voluntarily directing their own efforts towards organisational objectives.

McGregor believed that the Theory Y assumptions encouraged positive behaviour, while Theory X managers were creating the very attitudes that they complained about. In other words, managerial style reflects managerial perceptions.

From George's point of view, most of his staff are reasonably good workers, as long you keep an eagle eye on them. The real sore thumb is Mike, highly intelligent, good at his job, but totally lacking in social skills. Whenever there is trouble about, it is a pound to a penny that Mike will be at the root of it.

As George has told his wife (several times): you can dream up all the theories you like, but at the end of the day the only way to deal with a person like Mike is to keep on top of him every moment of the day.

But is that really the best way to deal with 'difficult people'?

Problems and outcomes

NLP offers three vital observations which should be the foundation of every manager's portfolio of 'people skills':

- People will always do the best they can with the resources available to them.
- Every behaviour has a positive intention behind it.
- Every behaviour is valid in some context.

A company (or section, or department) where it is 'safe to make mistakes' is likely to foster greater employee loyalty, greater creativity and greater commercial success. Companies which run 'by the book', on the other hand, tend to be low in rapport, low in creativity and ultimately low in profitability.

So how can these presuppositions be put into practice?

Looking for problems

The 'traditional', 'tough', 'firm', 'no nonsense' style of management tackles 'problem' situations head on (not to say confrontationally) by asking the following five questions:

1. What is the problem?
2. How long has it been going on?
3. Whose fault is it?

4. Why hasn't someone done something about it?

5. Who is to blame (for not sorting it out)?

In the case of George and Mike, this approach will surely indicate that Mike is at fault, and that George had better do something about it.

So, now George can give Mike a good dressing down. But does this bring them any closer to a solution?

Outcomes that work

So far, not very good.

Maybe it's time to switch to Theory Y tactics? Unfortunately, as any experienced manager knows, there are some people who don't seem to respond to the Theory Y approach.

NLP offers a third option based on studying the required outcome rather than simply restating the problem. This process starts with a very different set of questions:

- What do you want?
- What will be different when you have the desired result? (What will you see, hear and/or feel that will let you know that things have changed?)
- What resources are already available to you which will help you to achieve the result you desire?
- What other resources can you draw on?
- What is the next step?

This new way of viewing the situation moves from generalities to specifics, and allows us to find answers rather than getting fixated on the problem:

- Determine a suitable outcome (a smoothly running section with everyone getting on together).
- Describe how things will be when the situation is resolved (this implies that a solution exists and will be implemented).
- If we accept that Mike is doing the best he can with the resources available to him, then the first step must be to find out what the situation looks like to Mike. Maybe he knows there is a problem and would jump at the chance of some

help. On the other hand, he may think that everyone else is at fault. Either way, it would be a good idea to find out what resources Mike himself can bring to the situation.

- Assigning blame is as irrelevant to good management as finding fault. Is George more interested in finding a solution, or in giving Mike 'a taste of his own medicine'? Depending on Mike's attitude, this step involves deciding what outside resources are needed, and who is going to provide them (Mike, the company or both)?
- Finally, what are George and Mike actually going to do? Whatever solution the two men arrive at, the important thing is to start implementing it as soon as possible.

Looking for outcomes usually means talking things through and giving guidance. Not many managers have any training in this area, and the whole process will undoubtedly take up more time and thought, as against simply making threatening noises. Still, it really is the only practical way of achieving effective solutions.

The alternative is well illustrated by an incident where a young woman had been accused of acting in a disruptive manner at work. The entire disciplinary procedure for this case involved five managers, more than 35 man hours, and six quite gruelling interviews. The young woman subsequently wrote a letter to each manager, outlining ways in which she could improve her social skills. She received just one reply – three weeks later.

In your estimation, is the culture in that company based on finding solutions or on finding problems?

Hidden commands

The phenomenon of inadvertent hypnosis, or subliminal commands (Chapter 8), is particularly relevant to the disciplinary procedure. Consider the following example:

> After being reprimanded over some matter, an employee was told by their manager: 'And if anything like this happens again it will be regarded as very serious indeed'.

This typical warning seems straightforward enough yet it actually includes some very negative hidden messages:

- 'I don't trust you to learn from this experience' (judgement - manager to employee).
- 'I expect this person to offend again' (programmed expectations – manager to self).
- 'Live up to my expectations – go and reoffend' (implied command – manager to employee).

These messages have added power because they are effectively 'subliminal' (insinuated but not overtly stated) and therefore do not allow for an open discussion of their validity.

The fear of falling

It might be noted here that bullying, in whatever form, also has a subliminal foundation. That is to say, bullying invariably grows out of the bully's (unconscious and unadmitted) feelings of inadequacy and a fear of losing control rather than a direct wish to inflict pain and suffering on the person being bullied.

Employers who encourage a 'macho' culture, or are inclined to tolerate bullying, including overly severe and inflexible disciplinary procedures, may want to consider the negative consequences of such a culture on employee performance:

- Employees revert to 'tried and trusted' patterns of behaviour (bad for creativity and ability to handle change).
- Employees find it difficult to recognise underlying relationships and patterns (bad for maintaining coherent activities).
- Employees show reduced powers of memory and 'higher order' thinking skills (bad for company performance).
- Employees tend to overreact to events in the workplace (bad for employee/employee, employee/customer and employee/management relationships).

In short, bullying is not only morally unacceptable, in the long term it can become a very real threat to a company's ability to survive.

CHAPTER 17
Appraisals

What's the point?

It might seem obvious that the yearly or half-yearly round of appraisal interviews best serves the needs of company and employees alike when the result is a more highly motivated workforce with a clear notion of how each person will raise their level of achievement in the year to come.

So isn't it strange that in so many companies the appraisal interview is surrounded by FUD — Fear, Uncertainty and Doubt!

> In an effective appraisal procedure, both parties are left with the feeling that they have achieved a win/win result.

A key factor will be the ability of the appraiser to frame a clear outcome (Chapter 4), in which performance is measured against clearly defined, *mutually understood* expectations.

Perceptions and expectations

There is a famous experiment involving school teachers which shows very clearly how outcomes are moulded by our perceptions and our expectations (Chapter 2).

The teachers are told that a group of new students are either very eager and smart, or lazy and not very clever. In reality, the students are selected so that the two groups are evenly matched and about average in both attitude and ability.

As you may have guessed, the teachers who have been told that they are dealing with above average students report that their group are good workers and above average achievers. The teachers who think they are dealing with a group of problem students, however, find that the students' behaviour, both personal and academic, is significantly below average.

What is not so easy to anticipate is the fact that many of the allegedly above average students actually do begin to achieve above average results, while some of the so-called under-achievers begin to slip below their normal level of achievement.

If you look for people's faults, you will certainly find much to criticise, since none of us is perfect.

If you look for the good in people, you will certainly find much to praise, since most of us strive to do our best with the resources available to us.

Onwards and upwards

As we've already said, an effective appraisal process must be based on positive, clearly defined, appropriate outcomes, having the intention of moving things 'onwards and upwards' rather than dwelling on the past.

Echoing a point made in the last chapter, three principles apply to all human behaviour:

1. Every action has a positive intention behind it.
2. Everyone has all the resources they need.
3. People can only (consciously) use the resources they know that they have, and which they know how to use.

If we expand on these basic themes:

- People in a psychologically sound state of mind seldom if ever deliberately set out to fail or cause trouble. So reviewing the past year to pick over the mistakes, and worse yet, offering criticism without also providing concrete suggestions for improvement is, at best, pointless.

  The most realistic response to unwanted behaviour is to look for the good intention – and show the person how to achieve that intention in a more effective manner by helping them to become aware of a wider range of options.
- A manager's job is to manage, ensuring that his subordinates have whatever resources they need to do their jobs. The difference between a poor manager and a good manager is often as simple as the difference between:

  a) Assuming that people '*should* know better', and
  b) Helping each employee in whatever way is necessary for their success.

  It is interesting that some companies are now using staff appraisals as a way of assessing managerial performance!
- Having a resource, knowing that you have that resource, and knowing how to use that resource can be three quite separate conditions. An effective appraisal will include:
  - determining what resources an employee needs to fulfil their assignments, plus any resources they would like to possess (more or less relevant to the work situation[1])
  - identifying those resources which the employee does not consciously possess
  - drawing up a plan that will allow the employee to 'acquire' the additional resources, including on-the-job experience, formal training, self-managed learning, etc.

In short, the simple truth is that people succeed best when they are helped, encouraged and, above all, *allowed* to succeed.

---

[1] Various studies have shown that employee performance tends to be enhanced by learning in general, not only by the study of topics directly related to the company's main business.

CHAPTER 18
Motivation

Where there's a way

Years ago, one of the managers I was working with at the time came back from an interpersonal skills workshop and announced that he had made a major discovery: 'You can't motivate other people, and it's a waste of time trying'.

And he was absolutely right – and absolutely wrong!

If motivating someone means getting them so fired up that they will work flat out for the next 50 years with no further intervention, then no, you cannot motivate another person.

If, on the other hand, we're talking about understanding what gets another person excited, or turned off, so that we can encourage them to follow or avoid a certain course of action then we certainly can motivate other people quite effectively. What we need to know is which meta programs that person works to in a given situation and then frame our communication accordingly.

> Meta programs, like most other ideas in NLP, demonstrate the key fact that we create the best kind of interaction and co-operation when we deal with people as they *are* – not as we think they ought to be.

In this chapter we will restrict ourselves to six of the most frequently encountered meta programs, plus the modal operators mentioned in Chapter 10.

Towards – Away

When someone says: 'I want/don't want to do this *because ...*' listen very carefully to what comes next – it will tell you whether (in that particular context) their motivation is to work *towards* or *away from* the stated goal.

A Towards person thinks in positive terms: 'I want', 'I will', 'I can'. They have an image in their mind of what they want and they move more or less directly towards the realisation of their goals. If the Towards attitude is too strong it can seem aggressive and insensitive rather than assertive.

An Away person, on the other hand, thinks in negative terms: 'I don't want', 'I won't', 'I can't'. They are much clearer about what they are trying to avoid than about what they want to achieve, and this inability to express a positive desire can make it hard to formulate any kind of outcome (Chapter 4).

For motivation purposes, a Towards person needs to be pointed in the right direction and given their head (with some discreet checking from time to time to ensure that they stay on course).

An Away person can be motivated by threats, but take care, if the threats become too intense they may become afraid to do anything at all.

Options – Procedures

As the names suggest, an Options person thrives in a setting where they have freedom of choice, while Procedures people prefer to follow tried and tested lines of action.

Many Options people have a strong streak of creativity, which they may find difficult to control. They dislike following standard procedures, preferring to find their own way from A to B, quite possibly with diversions to C, D, E and F.

A Procedures person is happiest when surrounded by standards and a clearly defined course of action. In contrast to the Options person, they find choices distracting, and, given half a chance, they will follow a set policy to the bitter end, often with no regard for the consequences. The 'Jobsworth' ('I can't do that, it's more than my job's worth!') is an extreme version of the Procedures person. Bob, in the example on page 13, was certainly in 'procedures mode' in that particular context.

An Options person really doesn't need motivating as self-motivation is one of their main strengths; rather, they need to be kept firmly (but not too obviously) on track.

A Procedures person is best motivated by giving detailed instructions, minimising the element of choice and giving praise for their adherence to the standard procedures.

Proactive – Reactive

Proactive people are the ultimate self-motivators, the people who are regularly one step ahead of their colleagues. On the downside, they will often ignore the analysis and planning which is needed when making important decisions.

Reactive people are often noted for their love of collecting information and careful planning before doing almost anything at all. When Procedures people behave this way it is because they like to follow clearly defined pathways. Reactive people use these activities as delaying tactics because they would really rather do nothing at all. (Reactive people usually behave this way in order to avoid commitment and responsibility, not because they are lazy.)

Like Options people, Proactives need very little motivation, although they can be turned off if their initiatives are rejected or overly criticised. Reactive people work best in group situations, where they have very little responsibility, and when they have a clear idea of what they are required to do and why.

Incidentally, being proactive certainly isn't the best choice in every situation. Working in almost any kind of request-driven support role (a technical helpdesk, for example) would be most Proactives' idea of hell!

Convincer mode

How many times do you have to see something in order to be convinced that it is true? For example, if you were thinking of investing money in a business, how many times would you need to see details of that business to be convinced that it was a good investment?

For this meta program, instead of a continuous range of possible answers, four main groups have been identified:

1. *Automatic*: these people make up their minds in no time flat, often on very little information.
2. *Several times*: people in this group need to see the evidence several times over, although the precise number (usually less than ten) will vary depending on the person and the situation.
3. *Consistent*: these people are never entirely convinced and need constant proof that their original decision was correct.
4. *Period of time*: people in this group need to have things repeated over a given period rather than on a specific number of occasions. Here, too, the precise length of time may vary according to the person and the situation.

Sameness – Difference

Look at the pattern below and, as quickly as you can, write down a brief description of how the shapes are related.

Some people notice that all three shapes are the same, possibly with the qualification that the triangle in the centre is upside down. To Sameness people, the similarity they see in the world around them is more important than the differences, although they may acknowledge the differences as an afterthought.

Differences people, however, will note the differences before anything else, even if they then go on to notice similarities. These people might describe the figure thus: 'Two shapes are pointing upwards, and the middle shape is pointing downwards (all three shapes are triangles)'.

A third, relatively uncommon group of people, see the white V shape between the triangles before they see anything else.

Conventional Sameness–Difference people can be described using a four-step scale, with Sameness people and Difference people in positions one and four, with the qualified Sameness and qualified Difference people in places two and three respectively.

As far as motivation is concerned, Sameness people have very little interest in newness or innovation for its own sake. They naturally respond to conformity, traditional standards and ways of doing things, and so on.

Difference people, and the two 'with qualification' groups, incline towards concepts of 'newness', 'freshness', 'improvement' and 'progress' (try watching TV advertisements with this thought in mind!). The closer you get to the unqualified 'difference' group, the greater the attraction of newness and innovation for its own sake.

The final group (those who see the V-shape between the triangles) tend to be rather more unconventional and pioneering in their views, and do not fit neatly into the sameness–difference continuum. For want of a better description, we might regard them as being an extremely independent variation on the 'differences' mentality.

Internal – External
Sometimes referred to as the Frame of Reference filter, the Internal/External meta program is concerned with how people make judgements about their own actions. If you ask someone: 'How do you know when you've done well at a given task?', they may answer that they go by other people's reactions (eg peer pressure) or that they have some kind of internal yardstick.

The two basic positions are actually part of a much broader spectrum which includes at least five options:

1. External reference
2. External reference with internal check
3. Balanced
4. Internal reference with external check
5. Internal reference.

People with a significant element of external reference are relatively easy to motivate since your approval, or disapproval, will directly affect their perception of whether they are performing well. Indeed, they can sometimes seem over-responsive, because Externals often hear other people's input, even mild suggestions or queries, as commands.

A person with an internal frame of reference is really only interested in his own opinions. Where an External hears input as commands, an Internal person hears external input, even direct commands, as mere information. These people may be hard to motivate unless you frame your approach in the appropriate terms (see Modal Operators below).

Gentle persuasion

It is especially important, when discussing motivation, to remember that manipulation invariably fails, sooner or later.

The basic guidelines described in this chapter will only be truly effective when they are used to the benefit of the person *being* motivated, as well as for the person or organisation *doing* the motivating. Advertising agency people, for example, are extremely adept at using the various meta programs to stimulate customer interest in the products they publicise. Yet even the most sophisticated advertisements have a strictly limited effect and lifespan when they pretend to be addressing the real needs of the customer, but are primarily designed to serve the short-term interests of the manufacturer.

Modal operators

These motivating/demotivating phrases are often incredibly powerful, purely because they are habitual. A person can learn a modal operator in their childhood and go on using it for life, never questioning whether it has outlasted its usefulness.

A routine exercise for spotting and dealing with modal operators and similar auditory misinformation is given in Chapter 19. The most frequently encountered operators are:

- Can – Can't
- Could – Couldn't
- Have to – Don't have to
- Must – Must not (mustn't)
- Necessary – Not necessary (unnecessary)
- Need to – Don't need to
- Ought – Ought not
- Possible – Impossible
- Should – Shouldn't
- Will – Won't
- Would – Wouldn't.

Obviously, you can only use these operators for motivating someone if you already know which pair(s) of operators has significance for them, but they may well give you this information if you simply listen to the particular form of words they use. Thus, if you suggest a certain course of action, and the reply comes back: 'I don't think so – it looks impossible', you won't get far with: 'But we must!' or 'Well, I really think you should'. A far more effective follow up would be: 'Okay, I can see why you might think it was impossible for some people, but for you I think it *would* be possible'.

Corporate meta programs
It is worth noting that meta programs can also be found as the foundations of company culture. A company which finds it difficult to be innovative may be locked into Procedures mode, whilst a company that is high on creativity, but is never more than a step away from bankruptcy, may be too heavily Options oriented. Likewise, a company with a genuine emphasis on personal development usually has a Towards culture, whilst an Away company is often characterised by the undue amount of 'firefighting' that goes on.

CHAPTER 19
Negotiations

Straight down the middle

A negotiation can be as immense in its purpose as the SALT talks between the USA and the USSR, or as minor as discussing whether your child can have extra pocket money.

As long as the people on one side of the deal want something from the people on the other side of the deal, and both sides are willing to discuss the issues with the intention of reaching an agreement, then you have the basis for negotiation.

The negotiating process can be broken down into five basic steps, which can be memorised using the word PENCE:

> Preparation
> Estimation
> Negotiation
> Consummation
> Evaluation

In other words, any serious negotiator will start by:

- Preparing her own position, and
- Estimating the most likely position of the other party.

These preparatory steps are followed by the actual negotiations (step 3), the decision to either reach an agreement, or agree to abandon the negotiation process (step 4), and the post-negotiation evaluation stage (step 5).

The preparation

The foundation to any good negotiating strategy is to have an unclouded view of your own outcome(s). Not just 'I want', but clear definitions of:

1. Your ideal outcome.
2. The outcome that you expect to arrive at (approximately).
3. The least satisfactory result that you are prepared to accept.

You may, in fact, draw up several different versions of step 3, in order of acceptability. These positions are often referred to as BATNAs (*Best Alternative to a Negotiated Agreement*, or *Best Alternative to a Non-Agreement*).

The other man's shoes

It is also useful to get some idea of the position(s) the other party are likely to adopt. If you are dealing with a team you have faced before, this stage should be relatively easy. If they are complete unknowns, however, it can pay dividends to brainstorm the positions they *might* take, and work out your responses.

In both cases, however, you must bear in mind that you can never be entirely sure what someone is going to do until after they have done it. Whatever guesses you come up with, be prepared to throw every single one overboard, if necessary, once the negotiations start.

How to cut a dovetail

The most successful negotiations are those where the two sides work together to reach a mutually acceptable outcome (a 'win-win' result).

To reach such a result you will need to establish a good rapport (Chapter 5), and then to introduce the notion of working as a partnership rather than staging a war of attrition. It may be a novel idea to some people, but if you have indeed established a good rapport, it should prove acceptable.

This 'dovetailing of outcomes' is made possible when both parties reach agreement on a point of common interest as the basis for the negotiations. It may be necessary to chunk up and down (Chapter 11) from your opening positions to find this common point, but it will be worth the time and effort in terms of reducing the number of 'red herrings' and hidden agendas that occur during the rest of the negotiating process.

Although sharing a common outcome can help negotiations along, do remember how fallible the human memory can be. In other words, work together, emphasise areas of agreement whenever they arise, and make sure that every point agreed on verbally is fully documented and signed. Do this as you go along, before people have time to forget what has been said.

Congruency and other ways to make a point

Staying congruent (Chapter 13) during the negotiating process is a very necessary skill. Well-constructed negotiating teams invariably include a 'Differences' person (Chapter 18) who will be particularly aware of any incongruence in both your team and in individual team members.

When you want to 'sell' a point, especially if you expect a certain amount of resistance, always state the reasons first and then follow up with the proposal. If you put the proposal first, people won't hear your justification because they will be too busy running through all the objections they can think up (Chapter 9).

Metaphors

As described in Chapter 12, metaphors are an excellent way of getting your message across in a non-confrontational manner. They are also something to be regarded with the deepest suspicion when you are on the receiving end!

So how might you use metaphors in a negotiating situation? As a simple example, they can be used to indicate your own ideas about how the negotiating process should proceed:

We had a situation like this not long ago, and the customer suggested that we do x, y and z, and sure enough we got the whole deal sewn up in next to no time. And everyone was totally satisfied with the result.

or to reject a proposal without making it personal:

That reminds me of the time we were in negotiation with ABC Inc. They made a proposal much like the one you just put forward. We weren't entirely convinced that it was the best solution, but we make it a rule to respect the customer's decision. When we delivered the finished article they realised that it really wasn't what they wanted after all.
Now, how do you want to handle this ...?

Notice that the responsibility always rests with someone else in these stories (so you can't possibly be accused of saying 'We know best'), with you and/or your company appearing to be the epitome of reasonable co-operation.

Specify to clarify

Just how often do we send or receive generalised statements as though they were precise descriptions (Chapter 11)?

A: 'We must have guaranteed delivery by the end of June.'
B: 'No problem.'

Two months later:

A: 'Your delivery was late!'
B: 'No it wasn't. The goods reached you at 12:30pm on June 30th!'
A: 'That's what I mean. We said "by" the end of the month, not "at" the end of the month.'

The table below shows the five main areas where significant generalisations may occur, and the (optional) response to gain greater clarity.

It is important, in a business context, to recognise the difference between situations where a 'fuzzy' comment needs to be made quite clear and precise, and times when a vague statement or undertaking is, for the moment at least, entirely acceptable.

Generalisation	Example	Response
Comparisons	'This is the *best* deal you'll get'	Compared to what? How 'good' is best?
Unspecified nouns	'And we'll throw in some *transport*'	What 'transport' – a car, a truck, a bicycle? What make? How new is it? What condition is it in?
Unspecified verbs	'We will *improve* the delivery procedure'	Starting when? In what way? To what degree? Will it be an improvement that is of benefit to the customer?
'Rules'	'We *can't* do that!'	Why not? Who says you can't? What will happen if you do? Do you mean 'can't', or 'won't'?
Unqualified absolutes	'*Everyone* knows ...'	Everyone? Is that everyone in your company? In the country? In the world? Or everyone named Smith?

Of course, you don't have to wait until you're in a serious business situation before you start to look out for these 'sleights of tongue'. On the contrary, it is to your advantage to practise your listening skills by paying greater attention to the conversations going on all around you in the everyday world. Every conversation, whether you're involved or just listening in, is a 'safe' opportunity for you to develop an instinct for when you need to prompt for greater clarity and when you can allow a generalisation to go unchallenged.

CHAPTER 20
Sales

It's the way that you do it

One of the current business buzzwords is 'differentiation' — the process of making your own product or service stand out from all of its (very similar) rivals. What few professional service businesses seem to understand is that differentiation has very little to do with the product as such. When you are competing in a market full of nearly identical products, there's little mileage in stressing the negligible differences between one product and another. It is usually better to concentrate on the 'halo' around your product — the associations which will make that item or service *appear* to be more desirable.

Most people, from the loftiest CEO to the typical 'man in the street', are essentially creatures of habit. They develop certain buying patterns and are unlikely to change those patterns without a very good reason. The reason, moreover, is likely to be personal rather than business-oriented. (In a recent study, 76 per cent of the companies which changed suppliers had done so because the relationship with the supplier's representative had broken down in some way.)

However unbusinesslike it may seem, in a selling situation your 'personal' link to the customer matters far more than mere technical details (Chapter 5).

Believe it or not, the fact that your product or service is

genuinely superior to everything else on the market is not necessarily what your customer wants to hear.

To tell or not to tell

As we saw in Chapter 2, everyone has their own 'world view', which means that any person you are selling to will have his own individual set of reasons for buying, or not buying, whatever you are selling.

So, if you go into a selling situation and immediately start to tell the customer about your product or service (hereafter I'll use the word 'product' to refer to both) then you will be selling, at best, to some mythical 'Mr Average', or, at worst, to yourself. That is to say, you will be telling the customer what you believe they ought to want to hear, or you are telling them what *you* would want to hear.

In neither case are you treating the customer as a real person.

The person asking the questions controls the conversation.

Features and benefits

In order to enter your customer's world, which is, after all, where the sale will actually take place, you must ask questions which will encourage the customer to tell you what you really need to know. These questions need to be simple and precise:

'What did you like most about your last fleet car supplier?'
'Is there any way in which they could have given better service?'
'What did you least like about XYZ Training Ltd?'
'In what way did they fail to meet your training needs?'

Once you have a clear *idea* of what the customer actually wants from the product you are selling, you can frame your sales pitch to show how specific 'features' of your product can *benefit* the customer by answering specific needs. Incidentally, if you can't match a particular need, or if there are features of your product which don't relate to any of the customer's declared needs, leave that information out of your presentation. I repeat: no matter how many wonderful bells and whistles your product may have, the customer will only buy, and be satisfied with, what the *customer* actually wants.

How, then, can you help the customer to find out what they really want? This question brings us back to the subject of PTSs (Primary Thinking Styles – Chapters 4 and 14).

Selling to visual customers

Even when you think you know what they want, trying to *tell* Visual customers or clients what your product can do for them will be a total waste of time. Visual customers want to *see* what they're getting for their money, be it a car, a holiday, a new pair of shoes or a computer upgrade.

Be prepared to be patient going into the sale – Visuals often want to literally view all the alternatives before making a final decision. Give them the time they want, and don't try to talk to them until they've reached the 'short-list' stage, at which point you can help the process along by asking questions that stimulate visual images:

'Can't you see yourself lying on that beautiful golden beach?'
'Isn't that a good-looking car?'
'Just imagine the other drivers trying not to stare as you glide down the motorway.'

When Visual customers do come to a decision, they usually do so quickly and with conviction (they have finally built a mental picture which looks right). Avoid too much chit chat. Disturb that mental image and you may literally talk yourself out of a sale.

Finally, if Visual customers aren't ready to make an on-the-spot commitment, make sure you give them some kind of visual reminder to take away with them.

Selling to auditory customers

It might seem logical to suppose that the best way to sell to Auditory customers would be by talking about your product, yet in practice exactly the opposite is true. It is especially important that you give Auditory customers as much opportunity as possible to talk to you.

As soon as Auditories begin to interrupt or raise their voices, you know that they have started an internal review of the sale. Listen carefully and they will tell you everything you need to know to complete a mutually satisfactory transaction – gems such as: When they last made a similar purchase, and, even more importantly: What triggered their decision on that previous occasion.

Be prepared to answer questions, but remember that the Auditory's most effective salesperson is her own voice. If they start to repeat themselves then the sale probably isn't happening. In this case, listen carefully to what they are saying (to find out where the barrier is), then reframe the barrier (Chapter 9) to allow the sale to progress.

Selling to kinaesthetic customers

Making a sale to a kinaesthetically oriented customer or client can be very easy and very difficult – and both in the same transaction.

The process is easy in so far as Kinaesthetics readily respond to emotionally charged presentations and to 'hands-on' experience of the product – as long as the salesperson's enthusiasm doesn't become a hustle.

The bad news is that Kinaesthetics buy in response to their feelings and are quite likely to change their minds about their purchase just as soon as the accompanying emotion fades away. When this happens, they will not necessarily regret having bought the item (although they are the group most likely to suffer 'buyer's remorse'). Rather, they will start to question whether they got a good deal, whether the purchase was really necessary, and so on. (This indecision is even more likely if anyone else questions them about their purchase.)

In order to minimise the effects of this 'aftershock' syndrome, it is necessary to provide built-in reassurance.

IBM used to have a slogan along the lines of: 'No one ever got fired for buying IBM.' True or not, the effect of the slogan was to reassure Kinaesthetics that they had made the right choice by redirecting their fears towards the possible consequences of any alternative action (ie 'buying from our competitors could seriously damage your career').

Likewise, the documentation which accompanies many electrical goods congratulating the customer on their wise choice and asking them to register for after-sales support is an excellent way of reassuring Kinaesthetics and impulse buyers that they have made the right decision.

Selling to groups

You may be thinking that this is fine for sales to individual customers, but not much use when dealing with *groups* of customers. In practice, the information is equally valid in both situations. After all, a group is comprised of individuals, so you still need to deal with individual PTSs. The only difference when dealing with a group is that you need to use your sensory acuity to single out the key member(s) of the group and identify their PTS(s). Then weight your sales presentation accordingly.

Watch for the person or people who seem most at ease, who clearly are not afraid to express an opinion, who are the focus of attention for the rest of the group, and so on. If you're still not sure who the key figures (ie decision makers) are, simply tailor your presentation to cover all three PTSs more or less equally. In this manner you are bound to be on the same wavelength with everyone in the audience at some time or other. It's not very scientific, but it is better than achieving no rapport at all.

CHAPTER 21
Meetings

What are we here for?

As we've seen throughout this introduction to NLP, it is relevant to every area of business activity, and particularly to those events where communication is the primary purpose of the activity.

It would be easy, then, to write a complete book just on the application of NLP in meetings. Unfortunately, we don't have room to do that, so this chapter will concentrate on the six major steps that comprise any meeting – always assuming that a meeting is the best way of achieving your outcome(s):

> Specify the outcome(s)
> Agree the evidence
> Confirm the outcome(s)
> Use sensory acuity
> Summarise important decisions
> Agree action

Specify the outcome(s)

Generally speaking, the agenda for a meeting indicates the topics to be discussed, but it does little or nothing to ensure the success of that meeting.

When we talk about the outcome(s) (Chapter 4) for a meeting, we are interested in what the discussion will lead to, not just where it starts out. In this way we give the meeting focus and direction, and avoid the all too common problem of entering into inevitably fruitless discussions.

Agree the evidence
There is a widely held belief that discussing what has to be done is a time-wasting exercise and the way to succeed is simply to 'get stuck in'. A number of studies have shown that this is simply not true. Indeed, it is possible to cut the total time taken to achieve a given result by as much as a third simply by discussing the task before any action is taken.

On this basis, discussing outcomes at the very start of a meeting is far from a waste of time. Likewise, there is value in agreeing how you will (jointly) know when you have satisfactorily achieved those outcomes before you actually try to reach any agreement.

Confirm the outcome(s)
The third (and final) step in the opening of a meeting is to confirm the outcomes that have been agreed upon, and what will have to be true in order to know that those outcomes have been achieved. This will be far more successful if the items in question are written down and circulated. If they can be sent out to be typed up while the meeting continues, so much the better.

Use sensory acuity
Throughout the course of the meeting, it is important to be alert to what is really going on (that is, be aware of what people do – don't depend on what they say). If someone says they agree on a particular point, but shows non-verbal evidence of confusion or doubt, be sure to deal with those non-verbal cues (Chapter 1) before the meeting is over, or the agreement you have achieved may be short-lived.

Do remember that different people have different convincer modes (Chapter 18) – one agreement does not (necessarily) a deal make.

Summarise important decisions
Just as you established solid confirmation of the outcome(s) for the meeting, make sure that all important decisions reached in the course of the meeting are summarised and agreed.

Summarising has the added advantage of being a good way of checking that you all agree not just on the wording but also on the meaning of each decision.

Agree action
Finally, agree on the action to be taken on the basis of the decisions that have been made. These actions should feature in the minutes when they are circulated to the participants so that everyone knows what's going on, who has responsibility for follow-up actions, and any disputes can be aired (and settled) as quickly as possible.

Challenge for relevance

Whenever (if ever) a meeting seems to be losing focus because someone is (in your opinion) going into too much detail, taking too broad an overview, or simply diverging from the point, be confident enough to firmly and politely challenge the speaker to explain what relevance their point has to the agreed outcome(s) for the meeting.

Having said that, do remember to challenge the point, not the person making the point. The aim is to keep the meeting on track, not to create friction. Remember, every action has a positive intention, and even the most irritating nit-picker may have a valid point to make.

CHAPTER 22
Honesty

Honesty is still the best policy

Having covered as many features of NLP as possible in this relatively short space I must make one thing perfectly clear: NLP, no matter how elegantly applied, can only make a 'real' difference to a company if it is accompanied by a large measure of truthfulness.

Culture shock

In Chapter 3, we talked about the fact that many companies have a credibility gap between their declared vision, mission, etc and the way that members of management actually behave.

Not surprisingly, a significant degree of incongruence at any level within a company tends to cause an equally significant amount of stress for most of the people at lower levels in the company hierarchy. (I say 'most' people because a person who has been at the receiving end of incongruent behaviour since childhood tends to develop a degree of tolerance).

In practice, if managers intend to follow a policy of being lean and mean they can actually *reduce* tension levels in their subordinates by being consistently open about their intentions.

I'm not suggesting that people will like this attitude any better, only that they will find it easier to live with.

Who needs to know?

We also talked, in Chapter 13, about so-called need-to-know management. There are a number of reasons behind this particular style of management, all of which are related to fear in some way. It may be the fear of losing face, when the real answer would be 'I can't tell you because I don't know', or it may be a fear of losing power – 'If I tell you what I know then you won't come to me every five minutes for instructions and advice, and I won't have anyone to boss around'.

Part of the solution to this situation is for companies to accept that the phrase 'I don't know' is a valid response (when it is true). Putting managers in the position of having to know, or at least pretend to know, everything about everything has become increasingly unrealistic over the last few decades.

By the same token, many managers need to be more open about what they are doing. As well as being open about not knowing some particular piece of information, they also need to abandon the secretive: 'Oh, I can't tell you that!', and the superior: 'That's not for me to say' in favour of a clear statement such as; 'I'm not going to tell you, because ...'

As I noted in my book on presentation skills, and as I still believe, most people are able to recognise, and are willing to accept, an honest version of 'I'm not going to tell you that'.

Incidentally, need-to-know managers might like to remember that, where no official explanation is available, the company grapevine is always waiting to fill the communication gap with a ripe collection of rumours and half truths.

Truth is a two-way street

Some time ago I came across a company which was trying to educate its people about the need to keep accurate figures on their time sheets so that projects could be more accurately budgeted and managed. Unfortunately, the company culture did not look kindly on those who made mistakes, so guess what – the same managers who openly passed down the message about accurate time sheets were also having quiet chats with their teams about recording minimum overtime so that they could bring their projects in on budget!

In another case, a senior manager introduced her own, unilateral version of 'upward' feedback. When I commented on her go ahead attitude she announced, with a wry smile, that she was only doing it so that her underlings could tell her, anonymously, what a ruthless bitch she was.

I suggested that this result might be seen as a self-fulfilling prophecy, given that she was getting exactly the response that she expected (see Chapter 16), to which she replied that she was ready to listen to what anybody wanted to say, as long as they presented it the right way. In my experience this attitude seldom, if ever, brings positive rewards.

> If you wait to hear information in a form that meets with your approval you may *never* hear anything you really need to hear.

Bridging the honesty gap

So, does NLP offer any solutions to the 'honesty gap'? It certainly does.

One of the most common reasons for a lack of openess in the workplace is plain, simple fear. Fear of upsetting other people's feelings, fear of being seen as something less than a 'good team player', fear of committing a 'career limiting' error of judgement.

If a solution is to be found and made to work then it must be at the company level. There must be a focused programme, championed by a very senior manager (at least), designed to help people to find and exercise interpersonal skills like creating rapport, building inner congruence, sensory acuity, negotiating skills, and so on and so on. As these skills start to become commonplace, so openness and truthfulness will also begin to emerge.

Will it happen overnight? No.

Will it be easy? Not until people see that the programme really is being supported from the top.

Will it be easy to implement? Probably not, unless appropriate professionals are brought in to design a workable programme and provide the necessary training.

Will it be worth the time and effort? How long can you go on with the situation you have now?

For specialist training and consultancy in business-related NLP, we recommend:

Pace Personal Development
Leroy House
436 Essex Road
London
N1 3QP

Telephone: 0171 704 0044

Basic NLP Terms Used In This Book

(Words in italics are described elsewhere in the list of terms.)

Anchor An 'anchor' is a link between an internal *state* and an external stimulus (eg a piece of music that recalls a past event).

Anchoring The process of creating an *anchor*. Anchors can be created deliberately or by chance. They can also be altered and even removed ('dissolved').

As if 1. An event can be dealt with through visualisation 'as if' it had actually happened.
2. There is proven value in adopting certain presuppositions 'as if' they are true, even though it hasn't been proved that they are universally true.

Associated To be 'associated' with a given event or memory is to view it as someone taking part in that event.
(See also *Dissociated*).

Auditory Someone whose PTS is sound.
(See also *Kinaesthetic*, *PTS* and *Visual*.)

Beliefs An idea about some aspect of ourselves or the external world which we hold to be true without necessarily having any supporting evidence – 'I've never tried it, I just know [ie *believe*] I won't like it'.
(See also *Values*.)

Chunk However many items of information a given person can handle as a single concept or idea.

Chunking 1. Dividing a large piece of information into smaller 'chunks'.
2. Moving from details to generalities ('chunking up') or vice versa ('chunking down').

Congruence (external) External congruence exists when your body language, vocal signals and verbal content all send the same message.
Being externally congruent is very closely related to your level of *internal congruence.*

Congruence (internal) Internal congruence exists when you are completely focused on the task in hand *and* you are comfortable with the situation (ie when all of your *parts* are in harmony).

Conscious That part of the mind which is immediately accessible. It is the conscious mind which can only handle seven items of information, plus or minus two.

Content In any communication, the 'content' is the message you are giving out − as distinct from other people's interpretation of your message.
(See also *Process* and *State*.)

Crossover mirroring Indirectly matching another person's body language − you scratch your neck, I rub my arm − usually as part of the process of establishing rapport.

Deletion The process of ignoring certain items of information about some event, person or thing (for *any* reason).
(See also *Distortion* and *Generalisation*.)

Dissociated To be dissociated from an event or memory is to view it as though watching it as an observer.
(See also *Associated*.)

Distortion The process of interpreting information so as to misrepresent external reality (for *any* reason).
(See also *Deletion* and *Generalisation*.)

Dovetailing (outcomes) Matching your outcome with that of another person so that both outcomes can be achieved as far as this is possible. Note that dovetailing implies reaching a reasonable compromise but does not require you to sacrifice your own interests in favour of the other party.

Frame The context within which a person, thing or event is *perceived*.

Generalisation The process of creating a general rule or assumption on the basis of a very limited amount of evidence.
(See also *Deletion* and *Distortion*.)

Kinaesthetic Someone whose *PTS* is feelings – both physical and emotional.
(See *Auditory*, *PTS* and *Visual*.)

Leading Doing something different from the person with whom you are communicating, usually after a period of *pacing*.

Mental map In this context, a mental representation of a person, event or thing. All mental maps are, by definition, incomplete and out of date. Nevertheless, they are the best information we have about *external reality*.

Matching Discreetly copying someone else's body language as part of the process of creating and maintaining *rapport* (you cross your arms – I cross my arms, etc).

Metaphor A story – based or partly based on real events or entirely fictional – designed to convey a message so that it will be more readily received by the listener.

Meta programs The internal filters which people use to judge the world around them and to determine their own behaviour.

Mirroring Synonymous with *matching*.

Modal operators Internal rules by which people govern their own behaviour and judge the behaviour of others.

Modelling A basic NLP skill, in this context modelling is the process of capturing the thoughts and actions which distinguish an expert in some field from someone who is merely competent. The information must be described in such a way that it is possible for other people to replicate the relevant elements in order to enhance their own skill level.

Outcome (well-formed) A goal or want which has been

- consciously and specifically defined
- in positive terms
- can be achieved by the individual setting the outcome with minimal external help
- and has no discernable detrimental consequences.

Pacing *Matching* and *mirroring* another person's body language to help build rapport, often prior to *leading*.

Perceptions Our conscious view of the external world. Our perceptions are largely shaped by our *beliefs, values* and expectations.

Process In any communication, the 'process' element is the way that you handle your side of the communication. (See also *Content* and *State*.)

PTS Primary (or Preferred) Thinking Style — *Auditory, Kinaesthetic, Visual*. The sense which we use most frequently in assessing and describing the external world.

Rapport A state of mutual trust and respect existing between two or more people. Rapport is the primary basis for all successful communications.

Reality (external) The totality of the universe outside our skins. Since nothing is completely knowable our view of external reality is always limited.

Reality (internal) Internal reality is what is 'real' to a given individual — their current *mental map* of external reality.

Reframe Taking an alternative view of some aspect of *reality* (internal or external), usually in order to make it easier to deal with.

Resource Any internal quality (confidence, humour, calmness, etc) which makes it easier to perform a required task.

Having a resource does not necessarily mean that we know that we have it, and even when we know that we have a particular resource we may still need time and guidance to learn how to use it effectively.

Resourceful state Being aware that you have, and know how to use, the *resources* required in a given situation.

Sensory acuity The skill of being sensitive to another person's non-verbal changes (rate of speech, skin colour, muscle tension, etc) which give clues to their mental activity.

State Your actual condition (emotional, physical and mental), appropriate or otherwise, at any particular moment in time. (See also *Content* and *Process*.)

Thinking (two-valued) Thinking based on the (usually incorrect) assumption that there are only two options in a given situation.

Thinking (multiple choice) Thinking based on the (usually correct) view that there are as many options in a given situation as you can think of – and then some.

Unconscious The part of your mind which you are not usually aware of. The unconscious mind can handle vast amounts of information and multiple activities simultaneously.
(See also *Conscious*.)

Visual Someone whose *PTS* is graphical (including both moving and still pictures).
(See also *Auditory*, *Kinaesthetic* and *PTS*.)

Values Filters we use to evaluate incoming messages about ourselves and the world around us — good/bad, worthwhile/worthless, and so on. Our values are normally closely tied to our *beliefs*.

Select Bibliography

Brooks, Michael, (1993) *The Power of Business Rapport*. HarperBusiness, Scranton, Pennsylvania.
Despite the overtones of instant gurudom and a certain amount of padding, this (imported) book is packed with useful information. Well worth reading if you can find a copy.

Johnson, Kerry, (1994) *Selling with NLP*. Nicholas Brealey, London.
Although rather narrow in focus, the writing is pacey and there is plenty of useful information.

Knight, Sue, (1995) *NLP at Work*. Nicholas Brealey, London.
Not as technically detailed as *Influencing with Integrity* (see below), but more accessible to the layman. Specifically aimed at the business market.

Laborde, Genie, (1987) *Influencing with Integrity*. Syntony Publishing, Palo Alto, California.
— (1988) *Fine Tune Your Brain*. Syntony Publishing, Palo Alto, California.
Both books present a combination of in-depth explanation and lots of decidedly weird graphics. As good as *Introducing NLP*, but more focused on practical issues. Not recommended for complete novices.

O'Connor, Joseph and Seymour, John, (1993) *Introducing NLP*. HarperCollins/Thorsons, 1993 (revised edn), London.
One of the best general introductions to the subject, although a little dry in style.

Further Reading from Kogan Page

Better Management Skills

This highly popular range of inexpensive paperbacks covers all areas of basic management. Practical, easy to read and instantly accessible, these guides will help managers to improve their business or communication skills. Those marked * are available on audio cassette.

The books in the series can be tailored to specific company requirements. For further details, please contact the publisher, Kogan Page, telephone 0171 278 0433, fax 0171 837 6348.

Be a Successful Supervisor
Be Positive
Building High Performance Teams
Business Creativity
Business Ethics
Business Etiquette
Coaching Your Employees
Conducting Effective Interviews
Counselling Your Staff
Creating a Learning Organisation
Creative Decision Making
Creative Thinking in Business
Delegating for Results
Develop Your Assertiveness

Effective Employee Participation
Effective Meeting Skills
Effective Networking for Professional Success
Effective Performance Appraisals*
Effective Presentation Skills
Empowering People
Empowerment
Facilitation Skills for Team Development
First Time Supervisor
Get Organised!
Goals and Goal Setting
How to Communicate Effectively*
How to Develop Assertiveness
How to Develop a Positive Attitude*
How to Improve Performance through Benchmarking
How to Manage Organisational Change
How to Motivate People*
How to Plan Your Competitive Strategy
How to Reward Your Staff
How to Understand Financial Statements
How to Write a Marketing Plan
How to Write a Staff Manual
Improving Relations at Work
Keeping Customers for Life
Leadership Skills for Women
Learning to Lead
Make Every Minute Count*
Making TQM Work
Managing Cultural Diversity at Work
Managing Disagreement Constructively
Managing Organisational Change
Managing Part Time Employees
Managing Quality Customer Service
Managing Your Boss
Marketing for Success
Memory Skills in Business
Mentoring
Negotiating Skills for Business

Office Management
Personnel Testing
Process Improvement
Project Management from Idea to Implementation
Prospecting
Quality Customer Service for Front Line Staff
Rate Your Skills as a Manager
Sales Training Basics
Self-Managing Teams
Selling Professionally
Successful Negotiation
Successful Presentation Skills
Successful Telephone Techniques
Systematic Problem Solving and Decision Making
Team Building
Training Methods that Work
The Woman Manager